Prize I, Second Edition

Copyright 2016

Acknowledgments

The list of people who have helped me write this book is very long but I am going to do my best to include all of them. Apologies are certainly in order for that person that I forgot.

Matt Oakes; Jeff Parks, Jim Seeley, Forrest Moore, Glen Bridges, Jeff May, Fred Turjan, Jason Wilde, Gene Kluck, Tyler Silcox, Larry Reeves, Matthew Beavers, Bryon Beaton, Ed Carney, Mark Heuer, Shane Loveland and Ron Nichols.

Cover

Judy vom Oechtringer-Forst's picture was provided by Roger M. Green; zwinger vom Elderbach.

How to Use This Book

Training a versatile hunting dog, especially for JGHV tests, is not a cookbook project. Instead, a balanced approach is essential. Every dog (and every trainer) has unique personalities and capabilities to learn. The key is to use Prize I as a guide but not a concrete formula.

Training one of these dogs is an exceptional experience; gratifying and rewarding. Yes, at times it is frustrating but patience and common sense will prevail. The journey should be viewed with a long-term perspective: Where am I going to be three years from now? Ten years from now. Training dogs is a process...not a "program".

Group sessions are important because you will often be hunting with other people's dogs and, certainly, at tests you will be around other dogs. Getting your dog used to the chaos of testing is best done at group training days.

Don't overlook positive reinforcement...treats, petting, and praise. While there's a place for correction, positive encouragement can work wonders once the dog knows what it is supposed to do.

So, use the book as a guide, a source of tips and a general resource. Keep it by your chair and thumb through it frequently. But, in the end, training is all about you and your dog; your relationship which should be fun and positive.

Note that there is no Table of Contents. Due to formatting issues with E-books, the page number for chapters is often incorrect. So, just flip through it to find the chapter and information you need. Sorry about that.

Prize I; Second Edition

Preface

There's only one thing two dog trainers agree on: a third one is doing it all wrong. It is understandable that opinions vary so much because trainers vary and dogs vary. There are dozens of dog training books on the market and they rarely offer a standardized protocol for all of the subjects a versatile hunting dog requires. The key is to determine the system that makes sense to you and you can actually implement. Then, stick with it. Problems occur when you try to mix different trainer/authors methods.

Your own personality can determine your success as a trainer and JGHV handler as much as your dog's character. Hot tempered, loud, impatient people rarely have a "good hand" with a dog. If you fit this description, work hard to become the gentle, patient, quiet trainer that is most often successful.

Learn to listen. Experienced versatile dog trainers talk about it regularly: the new handler who insists on doing it their way as opposed to the tactics that are proven to work. The classic example is throwing dummies for your puppy after serious training begins. Despite cautions not to do this, many people continue to toss dummies 20 yards out which just teaches the dog that that is as far as they need to go to look for a duck. Open your mind to more experienced trainers and do your best to follow their suggestions especially if you have trained other breeds in the past.

Chapter One: Choosing a Dog [3] [4]

I learned years ago that to train and eventually own a good hunting dog, well, you gotta start with a good puppy. For most of us, that means a puppy from a kennel that produces dogs that

1. Are smart, calm and easy to train
2. Pleasant to be around
3. Point upland birds
4. Retrieve waterfowl
5. Track down wounded game, e.g. a whitetail deer.

See, most of us have a job and really don't need a second one as a dog trainer. There are just so many hours in a day so a puppy that is responsive and quick to learn just makes the process easier. And, who doesn't like c-a-l-m? A quiet, noble dog that is compliant and fun to be around? So, as one talks to breeders, they will all have dogs that are accomplished hunters and will have passed some performance tests to be "breed certified" but do their dogs exhibit the other traits that make a dog a truly "versatile" animal? Those are questions that need to be asked.

Now, the cheapest and most certain way of getting a dog as described is to go to the bank and borrow some money and buy an adult, trained, finished dog. Trust me, that is the most direct, error-free, and least expensive way to get a good versatile dog. But, everyone wants a puppy don't they.

Breeders talk about their dog's "drive" to hunt. I do too. Heck, without desire to find game, you have a pet. But, is this drive linear in its desirability? No, too much desire can lead to uncontrollable hunting and, most certainly, to difficult training. So, a dog with substantial desire and drive is required but not a freakish level.

A good versatile dog has a demeanor of nobility. It has a "switch" that turns from this graciousness to a demon when it enters the field or water. That, my friends, is what we are looking for and it ain't easy to find. The optimal versatile hunting dog also connects well with people (and not just its owner). From hunting buddies to family members to judges at a JGHV test, the complete dog doesn't mind folks. This calm nature is crucial if the dog is to be a valuable companion afield or by the fire. This trait cannot be determined by test scores. In fact, some of the highest scoring dogs are not the composed type. One just has to observe, talk to others, and make an educated decision around the very important trait. Is calmness all genetic? No, socialization and training can help insure a dog's composure to a degree but it is much easier to achieve if the parents were poised, tranquil dogs. There is a very thin line between too much "go" and nervousness and a dog with less than optimal desire. In my experience, it is a lot more fun to own a calm, compliant dog.

The last characteristic is a natural desire to retrieve and bring game to hand. We will talk later in the book about Force Fetching which I believe in. But, over decades of selective breeding, it is possible to develop a strain of dogs that, at the least, will *require* FF'ing. Alas, this is the current protocol for most breeders. Force Fetching dogs, while essentially required, does lead us away from the dog that, really, did not need it. So, over time, we inadvertently have families of dogs that absolutely must be forced to get the retrieving dependability needed for a finished hunting dog. In the perfect world, we would be choosing dogs that have a natural desire to bring game to hand. So, as one looks at puppies, the question of how much effort was required to "force" the parents becomes germane. If the parents needed six months of professional training to get them through the various JGHV tests, you can expect a similar need in their offspring.

The Various Breeds

Pudelpointer

In the late 19th century, a fellow named Baron von Zedlitz began successfully mating Pointers to Poodles selecting for the best traits of each breed. The pointing traits of the Pointer combined with the intelligence and protective coat of the Poodle resulted in a versatile hunting breed. Many people think this was merely a simple cross of outstanding individual dogs of these two breeds, but it was more complex than that. The Barber—and ancestor of the Poodle—was used too. And, the pointers were the old German Pointer, an indigenous dog of the era. The original gene pool consisted of about 90 of these German Pointers and just seven of the Barber dogs.

The puppies from this original mating series was then crossed with English Pointers to produce what proved to be an ideal all-round gun dog. Once the pointing trait was instilled, breeders began focusing on retrieving and tracking to develop a true versatile hunting dog.

Pudelpointers are strong, sturdy dogs with rough coats and a docked tail. They are usually brown in color and have a fore-lock above their eyes.

Large Munsterlander

In the late 19th century, German hunting dog breeders began to organize the rather haphazard breeding of gun dogs and "clubs" formed around the various breeds. The German Long-Haired Pointer Club created strict regulations around a breed standard which included no black and white dogs. However, in the area around Munster, Germany, breeders ignored this code and bred for optimal performance instead of some color pattern. By 1919, they had formed their own club and named the breed after their homeland.

LM's have long, feathered coats and tails. They hunt, point and retrieve game. LM's are noted for their calm temperaments and gentle nature with children and other dogs.

Deutsch-Drahthaar

Like the other German-bred dogs the DD is an all-purpose hunting dog. It has a tough, bristly coat for protection against the elements. DD's are tall, robust dogs. During the 19th century, hunting dog breeding in Europe was random and several varieties of rough-haired breeds existed. Late in the century, attempts began to separate these breeds in a more organized fashion and the wire-haired ones were, at that time, less popular. In fact, this type dog came close to extinction. But, by the late 1800's DD breeders had gotten their act together and began decades of selective breeding to produce the modern Drahthaar, one of the premier versatile hunting dog breeds.

There is controversy around the origin of the breed. Was is the Kurzhaar x the Airedale or the Kurzhaar x the Griffon?

DD's thrive on hard work and do best in hard hunting homes. For many years, the DD was virtually unknown outside Germany but now is exported to many countries and continues to grow in numbers worldwide.

Deutsch-Langhaar

Although this breed resembles a modern setter, its appearance is deceptive. This breed is a true versatile. It is typically large (63-70 cm's at the shoulder). DL's trace their ancestry similar to all the German pointing breeds. Later, it is believed that other breeds e.g. the old Water Spaniel, Gordon and Irish Setters, etc. were introduced.

The ideal color is solid liver but many show liver roan in coat. DL's have long tails normally. This is one of the more rare German breeds but has always enjoyed a dedicated following. DL's appear regularly in JGHV tests in North America.

Deutsch-Kurzhaar

This aristocratic breed is the classic multi-talented versatile hunter. Although primarily a pointing dog, it will retrieve game from land or water, track game, and, to its fanciers is considered the perfect all-around gun dog. It was created in the 17th century by breeding the old Spanish Pointer, the ancestor of so many of the versatile breeds with other German hunting dogs. This produced a rather slow, plodding dog but breeders bred in English Pointer blood, which actually had the Spanish Pointer and Foxhound blood in it, to get a wider ranging, faster dog. Even then, DK breeders stressed the methodical, thorough search pattern needed for optimal hunting. By 1870, a Kurzhaar Stud Book had begun and serious standardization of the breed ensued.

Like many breeds, some kennels branched more to the show ring while hunters preferred a smaller, more agile dog. True JGHV tested DK's remain among the most popular versatile hunting dogs available.

Small Munsterlander

A more recent breed, it is a smaller version of the Large Munsterlander. Apart from its size, there is a color difference too. SM's are liver and white. This breed was created in the early 20th century by crossing LM's with spaniel type dogs. Despite this introduction of "flushing" blood, the SM is a pointing dog.

Due to its size, SM's make wonderful home companions as well as ardent pointers and retrievers.

1. Morris D. in Dogs, A Dictionary of Dog Breeds

Chapter Two: Stuff to Buy

Part of the fun (and expense!) of training a versatile hunting dog is accumulating stuff. And, there will be substantial purchases but your inventory can be spread over a year or two as you advance in the training process. Initially, you will need a leash. Early on, a simple, cheap one is sufficient. I like a plain rope with a chain choke collar attached. This arrangement can injure a puppy's windpipe if abused so be cautious with its use. Don't get in the habit of tugging the leash/collar device instead a quick snap is optimal.

A package of treats is important. There are several on the market but Bil-Jacs are nice as are Ivet treats. These treats keep well in your pocket and are about the right size for your puppy.

Eventually, you will need a Jaeger Lead; a complicated handle for your dog as he grows. Jaeger Leads are important because they allow you to loop one end around your body and attach the free end to the dog's collar. This allows you to have your hands free for shooting. There are dozens of Jaeger Leads available. The classic is the Altmoor Lead which is excellent but not available as of this printing. I also like the paracord ones made by Black River Precision in Bentonia MS. An internet search will provide lots of sources. Showing up at a test with a bona fide Jaeger lead shows preparation.

A JASA collar is another good investment. It is a large leather collar with "studs" on the inside. They come with either pointed studs or blunted ones. The blunted ones are preferable and will do the job. The JASA collar will be used in daily training around all the obedience subjects.

Be on lookout for some colored plastic clothes pins. I like the white ones but others will do. These will be used to mark your blood tracks during training. Also, pick up some little red or white "pom-poms"; small cotton balls about 1" in diameter. These can be handy for marking blood as you do your VGP blood track.

A small package of golf balls will be a good purchase. They will be used for the Blind Retrieve if you dog is not on its "A" game the day of the test and needs help locating the hidden duck.

A special leash for releasing your dog on drags is a good idea. There are many different formats but a simple piece of cord, ¼" in diameter that can simply be looped under the pup's collar is fine. When you release your dog on its drag, just hold on to one end and let loose the other so the dog can take off on the track without you struggling to unsnap a standard leash. I have a bolt-snap on mine that I click onto a belt loop. Then, I only have to worry about one end of it to hold to and loose.

A ventilated game bag for carrying birds to the field is an excellent purchase.

A "Quail-Condo" from Lion Country Supply (www.lcsupply.com) will allow you to keep a few quail at your house for training. While you are on their website, you might order the plans for a small "pigeon loft" which will hold 6-8 adult pigeons.

Pick up some small squeeze bottles for dispensing blood on a practice track. They need to hold about 8 ounces. And, be thinking about a supply of deer blood. A local deer processer can easily save you some. Just provide them with several gallon jugs for collection. Blood freezes well.

A nice canvas bag or a crate of some type to hold all your training gear will help you keep up with it.

Also, rig up two nice "drag strings" for use in dragging game during training. Most veterinary clinics have disposable nylon leashes that are cheap or free. Tie two together for a long drag string.

Obviously, you will need some type of crate for your dog to ride in and train out of. The ubiquitous airline shipping crate seems popular but will have to be replaced over time. And, there are currently several up-scale kennels available.

Plastic ducks with strings for long throws are nice and most people have a few. Be on lookout for a nice, white five-gallon bucket too. You can use this for initial blind retrieve training. A good supply of standard "dummies" is nice to have but you don't need dozens.

You might as well go ahead and build a "Fox in the Box" obstacle. The dimensions are in the VGPO Rule Book. Optimally, you will design the front side with removable boards so you can start short and gradually add height to the official level or even a little higher.

A duck pen will be convenient. You will either need to keep a few (3-4) live ducks on hand or have a ready supply within a few miles of your home. It is much easier to let someone else house them and just buy a duck or two all along. But, ducks can be hard to find hence you may need to keep some at home. They are a lot of trouble; require lots of water e.g. a child's swimming pool to play in; and they eat a lot! Confined ducks can get pretty nasty so find a safe, predator-secure area away from your house.

A used deep freeze is almost required. You will accumulate a lot of dead training game and it would be more appealing to keep it out of your family's food freezer.

An electronic training collar is a standard purchase. They come in many configurations and several brands. You need one with a variable intensity mode and both a "nick" button and a "continuous" button. The ones that have a buzzer or sound burst are not needed but a "beeper" to help you locate your dog is a nice addition. As far as brands, the two that I have found most useful are Tritronics and Dogtra. Many things can go wrong with an E-collar in the wrong hands but we will talk about their use later. A word about the combination GPS/training collar is in order. They are nice and I have one. In my hands, they are not as useful for daily training as the standard ones. But, due to the cost, you might consider just buying a Garmin or similar initially. They are wonderful tools when your dog is lost or out of sight for a long period.

Remote launchers are expensive but a great tool. Again, they can be misused so we will talk about them later too. They are worth the money but if you have a training partner that will help you regularly that can suffice. The noise created by the remote launcher can spook a pup, so, again, use caution and common sense. A less expensive alternative is the "step-on" bird trap. They are much cheaper and, in my hands, have been nearly as good. In early pointing training, it is nice to flush the bird before the dog points. Without an assistant, the only way I know to do this is with a remote launcher.

Everyone needs a whistle. A good dog trainer dons his or her whistle just like their underwear...every day. Never begin a training session without your whistle. So, what kind of whistle. Ideally, a "dual-tone" unit is purchased. However, a good one is hard to find. If you are a member of NADKC or have a friend that is, this organization had the classic Acme Dual-Tone whistle available on their website at one time. One side of the whistle is just a clear blast. This side is used for "Here". The other side has a pea in it to give the "triller" sound. This will be used for the "Halt" or "Down" command. It shows experience and knowledge if you have an Acme Dual-Tone around your neck.

For years, I trained without a Retrieve-R-Trainer, a device that will cast a dummy 80-100 yards. My rationale was that all retrieves in JGHV tests are "blinds" so why throw marks? It turns out that long marks actually help a dog learn to retrieve at a long distance even blinds. So, I eventually bought one and sure enough, I think it helps a dog learn that the duck is often w-a-y out there. In addition, these long swims help condition a dog for hunting or testing. By the way, get a thick glove to hold the thing when you fire it.

You need to begin building your library too. The Altmoor Puppy Manual is a standard purchase that almost everyone makes. I don't agree with everything in it, but I do strongly recommend you purchase this book. It is excellent overall.

It seems obvious, but for goodness sake buy the Rule Books (a VZPO and a VGPO). Don't try to prepare for the tests without a rule book.

Chapter Three: The Ahnentafel

The registration document is a crucially important piece of paper. It is considered by your registry as a true legal document and it certifies the actual owner of the individual dog. The actual format varies from breed to breed but generally, this explanation will address most of the versatile breeds. It is important that the Ahnentafel goes with the dog to any new owner. There is a four-generation pedigree on the reverse of the Ahnentafel and the front side provides a complete history of the dog's test scores, previous owners, and provides the certification or lack thereof of the dog's certification for breeding.

On the front, on the right side, you will find the dog's official name, its registration number (called a ZB-Nr) which reflects the tattoo in the dog's right ear. Its gender (*Geschlecht*), color (*Farbe*), and birthdate (*Wurfdatum*) along with the name and address of the breeder (*Zuchter*). Some dogs will have a long phrase, *aus auf Form und Leistung gepruften Eltern*, above their name. This certifies that the dog is the product of a Performance Mating, meaning that both parents were especially suitable for breeding.

Once the dog has been X-Rayed and the Veterinary Radiologist in Germany has inspected the images, the Breed Warden will stamp the Ahnentafel HD-free and ED-free if they have been certified free of these orthopedic conditions. If, for some reason, the dog is NOT suitable for breeding, the word *Zuchtverbot* will appear on the Ahnentafel.

There should be a sticker on the lower part of the Ahnentafel, which reflects the chip number installed in the dog as a puppy.

On the Left side of the front, there is a long paragraph that just states that the Ahnentafel is a legal document that should be protected from damage and kept in a secure place. Note that the official, registered name of the dog is to be used at all times. Any short, random call name the owner uses should not be noted on this paper.

There is often confusion around the German terms and the blanks to be completed. Here's a table that explains what goes where:

Tatowiert am: Date of the tattooing (in the European format: dd.mm.yyyy

Unterschrift des Zuchtbeauftragten: Signature of the Tattoo Agent

Abgegeben am: Date puppy transferred to new owner

An: Address of puppy buyer

Name und Anschrift des Kaufers: Name and signature of puppy buyer

Unterschrift d. Verkaufers: Signature of seller i.e. the Breeder

Below this information are the lines for the Senior Judge(s) to write the results of any and all JGHV tests the dog enters.

On the back of the Ahnentafel is a wealth of information about the dog and its parentage. The far left column identifies the actual parents of the dog. The mother is always on the top. As one reads across, less information is included but the names, etc. are shown.

In the parents "boxes", several odd-looking symbols are included. Here's a table that explains them:

/ means Toughness Certification

\ means Loud Hunter Certification

– means Dead Game Bayer

| means Dead Game Guide

Just below the parent's name, there are three kinds of notations. Every dog has a six-digit number called the ZB-Nr. which is simply the registration number and is the same as the number tattooed in the right ear. Next to this number, one may find some abbreviations like AH for Armbruster Halt Award, Vbr for Retrieve of Wounded Game and a Btr for Test of Retrieving Reliability.

To the right of the parent's name there may be a second number, five digits long and in bold type. This is the DGStB-Nr., the Studbook Number, assigned to dogs that have passed the VGP.

If the dog has been examined at a Breed Show, the next line will indicate that and an odd looking number like this appears: 212/16. This means the dog was number 212 in the Breeding Register and was born in 2016. The following lines explain the dog's Breed Show and various test scores. This number is commonly referred to as the "ZR Number". It is very important because, for all practical purposes, for a dog to be bred, it should have a "ZR Number".

Low in the box is listed the "ML" or mother line or the breed from which the dog was developed. PP is Pudlepointer, DK is Deutsch-Kurzhaar, GR is Griffon, and ST is Stichelhaar.

It is obvious that a fortune in information is available on an Ahnentafel and that the document should be kept in a special place protecting it against loss or damage.

Chapter Four: Training Philosophy

[*Much of the information in this chapter is gleaned from Robert Milner's Book: Absolutely Positively Gundog Training. It is available from Amazon and it is recommended that you actually purchase Robert's book for more detailed information about training philosophy.*]

I trained my first gundog, a Chesapeake Bay retriever, about 1975. Or, more accurately, I mis-trained her. Oh, she made a great duck dog but most of her skill was innate and was exhibited despite my clumsy attempts. She did eventually pass some easy tests held by the Memphis (TN) Retriever Club and, yes, she picked up a lot of ducks for me over her lifetime. But, looking back, she wasn't really a trained dog by modern definitions. Since that time, I, like most trainers have used tried and true methods of "compulsive" preparation; if they don't do it right, they get corrected and eventually, they comply to avoid this correction. Yes, it has worked.

But, there are newer ways that are gaining acceptance except among the most old-school of us. I am sure you've heard of "clicker training". It's not complicated. The dog gets a reward for good work and no reward for bad work. That's it. Now, your breeder may scoff at this approach and with some basis in truth. But, we are going to explore the subject and, at least, offer it as an option.

Back in the 1930's, a guy named B. F. Skinner wrote a huge book called "The Behavior of Organisms" and coined the phrase "operant conditioning". Skinner promoted the idea that one could make the world a better place if only rewards for correct behavior was employed. Most of his work was with pigeons and rats in a very controlled environment. A close inspection of Skinner's research finds lots of holes. He was, after all, a literature major not a scientist. Regardless, his work is often cited as the basis of reward for correct performance and evidence that correction is not necessary. He promoted "nice" training methods and opposed "unpleasant" tactics. While some of this training philosophy has its place, behavior like aggression, destruction of property, and unruliness just require correction. In the 1930's and 1940's, if an urban dog failed to respond to the Skinnerian tactics, the answer was "get rid of the dog". Essentially, Skinner recommended "reward good behavior and ignore bad behavior". Of course, out in the country, hunting dog trainers were not reading Skinner's work so they were using just the opposite methodology. I recall coon hunting with some fellows one night as a teenager when one of their dogs ran a deer for an hour. They finally caught the dog and took turns whipping it. Of course, the dog thought it was being punished for being caught; not running the deer. Neither training philosophy is optimal. My personal experience is that to develop the truly dependable versatile hunting dog, a combination of tactics is optimal. Let's see what it's all about. [9]

[9] Wilkes G. Internet blog. 2014.

Training Frequency

When I trained my first dog for JGHV tests, I was admonished that you need to train every day. In fact, a successful German trainer told me that he trained every afternoon after work religiously. So, I followed suit and, yes, it worked. I trained essentially six days a week for at least an hour. It was rigorous. But, after training several more dogs, I noticed that if I skipped a day or two, my dogs seemed to progress more rapidly! Over time, I adopted an "every other day" schedule and, frankly, in my experience, if I relegate the dog to even once a week hard training that proverbial "light bulb" seems to go off quicker.

As a result, I now keep sessions quite short and focused on one subject. This has led to the fastest overall success. Now, I do believe in training as part of my daily routine. For example, when I release a dog from her kennel, I use the word "Whoa" as I open the gate and make the dog stand still for a few seconds before giving the "OK" release. As I walk to the training area, I use this time to practice "Heel" either on or off leash. This allows me to get a lot done in a short time. Once I arrive at the area for say a Stobern or Down Stay, this meeting may last a little as ten minutes. There are exceptions of course; Live Duck Searches or even just Blind Retrieves which may take a while. In my experience, problems arise when one tries to cram a week's worth of training into a Saturday morning. It just overwhelms the dog. This concept was documented in a research project at the University of Copenhagen [6]. The scientists divided 44 dogs in to various groups and gave them all the same number of training sessions but they trained some of the dogs once or twice a week, some less and some dogs were trained every day. The group that was trained once or twice a week performed better than the other groups. Now, keep in mind, the dogs all received the same number of training sessions! So, if we accept this regimen, we have to realize that the entire training project will take longer. Regardless, in the final analysis, the dogs trained with breaks in their schedule, did perform better in the end. Optimally, we would provide structured training every other day focused on a single subject per session.

Now, the dogs in this study were in a controlled environment; kept in a kennel. A dog housed with the family will be exposed to lots of stimuli on a daily basis outside their formal training. While this can be advantageous, e.g. using your daily routine to teach Heel, Sit (with an implied Stay), Here, etc. it can also work against you as the dog is used to relaxed interaction with its owner and, suddenly, is asked to learn a new task in a "work" situation. That transition can be problematic for a dog sleeping on the sofa one minute and asked to do a Down Stay the next. Going from a happy, playful time with children to required behavior may prolong the training process.

2. Milner R; Absolutely Positively Gundog Training,

3. Demant H et al: The effect of frequency and duration of training sessions on acquisition and long-term memory in dogs, Helle Demant, Jan Ladewig, Thorsten J.S. Balsby and Torben Dabelsteen. Applied Animal Behavior Science, June 15, 2011.

Chapter Five: The Electronic Collar

In 2002, I attended a Rick Smith Training Clinic in Virginia. I sat on the back row and kept quiet although I probably had more experience with hunting dogs than any of the "students". One fellow, leading an Old Hemlock-type setter sat on the front row. When Rick got into use of the "Remote Training Collar" as the manufacturers like to call them, the setter guy asked "What if I don't want to use a shock collar?" As I recall, Rick replied "You are going to have lots of trouble."

Of course, hunting dogs were trained for decades before the E-collar was developed, so, yes, it is certainly possible. But, when you consider the distance between you and your puppy during training and hunting, some type of control is desirable other than a verbal command or certainly corporal discipline.

The first E-collar I used was a borrowed Tritronics with a 24 inch antenna and just one button: "High". I didn't accomplish much with it. I was totally ignorant of its use and, while I didn't ruin my Chessie, I sure didn't help her much either. Things are a lot different now. First, the devices are far advanced from the early 1970's. And, we've learned a lot more about dog training, E-collar usage, and caution with this tool.

For new dog handlers, the E-Collar can be a mysterious, intimidating tool. Let me say first that I am a proponent of the E-Collar. If you are not, then this section may seem prejudicial. I just believe that modern training tactics are better than what we did twenty years ago.

This instrument became popular in the 1960's and trainers have argued about it ever since. True enough, the early models were crude and really, didn't work well. There were stories of a collar not turning off after pressing a button and the poor dog suffered continual shocking for minutes on end. Plus, early on, trainers would use the collar to vent their anger and frustration with the dog pressing and re-pressing the button. This type of usage can ruin a dog.

The modern collar is an entirely different instrument. The major improvement is the variable levels of stimulation. Dogs vary in their sensitivity to electric shock and most dogs respond to very low settings; an option that wasn't available in the old collars. Also, modern collars have both momentary and continuous buttons. Some people like the tone feature which allows the trainer to give an auditory sound prior to electrical correction. In my hands, this feature has been of minimal to no value.

The E-collar can: send a negative message to your dog at a distance. It allows you do provide correctly timed correction. Hence, the E-collar really can only do two things: Enforce known commands and create places you want your dog to avoid at a distance, e.g. a road, a railroad track, the neighbor's sheep, or your wife's Pomeranian. But, this second function also becomes important in training for hunting. For example, your dog is sent on a Blind Retrieve during a training session and he's been doing these for a while. Instead of heading straight across to the hidden duck, it veers toward a nearby island. Light stimulation with a verbal "A-h-h-n-t" can encourage the successful route.

The E-collar cannot: teach a dog anything. If the pup doesn't know what to do before you correct him, he won't know afterwards either. The only exception to this is that tactic of avoiding a hazard.

Collar Conditioning is a term tossed around a lot with little understanding of how to do it. The simplest method is to start with a Bark Collar. See, this introduces the dog to electricity and it won't take him long to figure out that barking equals a "nick". While it is good to stop incessant kennel barking, really we are just introducing our new method of correction for later use. This allows any disturbing reaction to the stimulation to be overcome so that later, when you use your training collar, the pup won't freak out.

After the pup is used to the Bark Collar, you need to determine the correct level of stimulation needed for your individual dog. This varies tremendously from dog to dog and cannot be predicted by the dog's overall demeanor. Some of the gentlest dogs require substantial levels of stimulation while a knock-em down, wild thing may be very sensitive to electricity.

Put the collar on your pup and let him wear it around in the yard for a day or two to get used to the new device and its weight. Put him on leash and begin walking around. Starting at the very lowest setting, press the continuous button. Observe for a reaction like holding his head sideways, tilting his head, etc. If there's no reaction, go up one level at a time until you get some signs of stimulation. If the pup vocalizes, it is too hot. This establishes his "base level" which will suffice for 90% of your training. A few times, you may have to increase the level to communicate with the pup but most of the time, this lower level will be in order.

Next, you move to a simple command: Sit. Using the base level, start continuous stimulation just before you say Sit. Since he already knows this command, he will promptly sit. Immediately after he complies, stop the electricity. Thus, he begins to learn that the only way he can stop the stimulation is to comply with the command. Verbal praise and petting provide positive reinforcement after he sits. After several sessions doing this, just start the electricity a second or two before you say Sit. If he sits readily, he has gotten the message and understands how to turn the stimulation off.

Continue using this format around "Here", "Kennel" and other simple commands that he already knows. This way he learns that the electricity is not just tied to one command making it easier later to use the collar to correct many unwanted behaviors from chasing birds to failure to come to you. Once you reach this level, you can call your pup "collar conditioned".

A conversation with a field-trial retriever trainer may lead you to another approach in E-collar usage, i.e. using the highest setting the dog can stand without the dog totally quitting. This may be fine for the exactness required of field-trial retrievers but, frankly, is not needed for the versatile hunting dog tester/hunter. And, in the wrong hands can destroy a dog's natural ability to be a sound hunter. Hence, this method is not recommended.

Chapter Six: Pointing

> *"To many training routines have been conceived and written about with everything*
>
> *Present but the dog; as you will discover when you try them."*
>
> **--George Bird Evans**

Puppies should be introduced to birds, e.g. pigeons, <u>before</u> serious obedience work is begun. If you reverse this order and begin demanding strict obedience out of a puppy early in life, it will be less likely to show great enthusiasm for birds which is crucial to its development as a hunting dog. While the puppy is still a bit "wild", birds should be introduced. At this stage, I like a juvenile delinquent.

The last thing one wants is a dog that is spooked by its first bird experience. While this can be overcome, there is no reason to take two or three steps backward and have to re-train the dog to like birds. The best way to introduce birds to a 4 month old puppy is with a "locked-wing" pigeon. By placing the pigeon's wings in an intertwined fashion over its back with one wing "locked" around the other, the bird cannot flap its wings and startle the puppy. Spread the wings by holding the right wing in your left hand and the left wing in your right hand. Fold the left wing behind the right wing. Lock the elbow joint of the left wing over the elbow joint of the right wing. Now, the bird cannot fly or flap. While not really difficult to do, some practice is in order for "locking" the wings. Ideally, a corridor of temporary fencing will be constructed about 15 feet long by 6 feet wide. With the pup near you, just toss the locked wing bird to the other end of the fenced corridor. Generally, the puppy will run to it, smell it, maybe bark at it and eventually pick it up and drag it around. The fenced panels keep the puppy from running off with the bird so you can catch it easily and repeat the toss. Several days of exposure to the locked wing bird will help the puppy learn that "Hey, these birds are fun!" Once the puppy is enthusiastic about grabbing the pigeon, one can move to the "clipped wing bird".

A clipped wing bird can flap its wings and even fly a little bit but cannot fly off. There are several ways to alter the wings but the easiest is just some light weight tape wrapped around the long flight feathers on <u>both</u> wings. As an alternative, a water hose about 2 feet long can be fashioned with hobbles that attach to the bird's legs. These are available readymade for less than $10 from Lion Country Supply and are excellent tools. Leave the corridor behind and go to a wide open field where there are no trees nearby. Again, toss the bird out about twenty feet and let the pup see it land. The bird will walk around and as the puppy nears it, it will fly a few yards with the puppy chasing it or, with the hobbles on, you will have to toss it in the air. Eventually, it will catch the bird and hopefully bring it back near you so you can get the bird and repeat the drill. Repeat this drill for several days until the puppy truly loves chasing birds. Now, the dog has been correctly introduced to birds.

The next step is to encourage actual pointing which will occur after introduction to gunfire.

Here's the scenario that we assume: you pup is four months old; has been checked by your veterinarian and is current on vaccinations, parasite control, and is healthy. He's well socialized, comes when called with the command "Here", has been exposed to weeds, water, fields, trees, and is enjoying being a puppy and he's been exposed to birds, e.g. pigeons. He has a collar with your name on it and will walk on a leash.

Now, it's time to expose him to larger fields to expand his Search and learn to stay in touch with you. Just take them along for walks, again, primarily in large fields. The pup will find interesting scent all over the place which will gradually draw him further and further from you. If at all possible, don't whistle or call to the pup during these expeditions. We want the puppy to range far and wide without being "hacked" back in. Take the pup to a safe, road and hazard free area so it can range out without danger. While you don't need to work him on birds much at this point, providing one or two birds per trip will get him focused on birds instead of mice. No more than two birds per trip is optimal. Keep in mind, a four-month old puppy can catch sluggish pen-raised quail so try to avoid this if at all possible by hand selecting strong flying, wildish birds for these expeditions.

When they semi-point and quickly flush the bird, and are really chasing the bird aggressively, shoot a .22 crimp-style blank one time during the chase. Gradually, you can move to a .410 with light loads over a period of two weeks. Gun sensitivity is uncommon in the versatile breeds, but caution can prevent problems so use common sense. To move forward with real training, your pup needs to be fearless around gunfire. So, go slow and if the pup seems to notice the gunfire, let him chase some more and really get into it before using the .22 blanks again. At this point, it is crucial that you **say nothing!!** We are not teaching Whoa at this point!

After a week or two of these trips, it's time to shoot a bird for the puppy. Are you positive he likes gunfire? If so, kill a bird for him and let him pick it up, run around with it, and just get the taste of a bird. This teaches him that the bird is fun and can't hurt him. For goodness sake, don't get into a tug-of-war with the pup over the bird. Once you get your hands on him, just ease his mouth open and remove the bird.

Keep in mind, we really haven't said anything to the dog at this point. We are using a non-verbal training system at this point.

Gear: You only need three tools to work with pointing: a JASA collar (with blunt spikes), a 15-foot check cord, and an electronic training collar. Now, remote launchers are a nice tool but with a dependable assistant, can be excluded.

Real Training

Most of us don't live in an area where wild birds are plentiful. So, we are forced to use "tame" game for most of our training. Is this optimal? No, but the options are limited. It becomes all about pigeons. Pigeons are durable, they don't peck, and are easily kept. Ideally, you learn to trap wild pigeons around barns because they fly much better than pen-raised ones. However, lots of dogs have been trained with tame pigeons. You will need a nice place to keep them, called a "loft". Lion Country Supply has plans for a small coop which works for 6-7 birds.

There are two ways to "manage" pigeons during training; a remote-launcher or the "carded" bird with an assistant. Let's look at both methods.

The "carded" pigeon has a piece of corrugated cardboard, rectangular in shape and about 10" x 10" tied with some soft yarn to the pigeon's leg. You just punch a hole in the center of the card and push the yarn through the hole, tying a big knot on the end to prevent it coming through the small hole. The remainder, about 20 inches, is attached to the pigeon's leg. Don't use twine or cords because that will damage the bird's leg. Think soft. If you want the best "cards" in your training group, look for some Coroplast, a more durable material that sign makers use. I'm cheap, so I just use cut up boxes. You may have to experiment a bit with the actual size of the card depending on your pigeon's flight strength, their size, etc. Also, if you are training in a small field, a larger card will prevent a long flight to nearby trees. You can figure this out after a trip or two (after a few pigeons have been lost).

After insuring that the yarn will not pull through the hole, toss the bird and cardboard into some cover. Avoid walking all the way into the area because a good versatile puppy can track you right to the bird. We want the puppy to find the bird with its nose in the air. At times, the pigeon will fly before you return, so keep one eye on the area as you get your pup. This is actually a good thing normally because it avoids human scent around the bird.

When the pup points the bird, on a check cord, your assistant will flush the bird probably by tossing it in air. The pigeon will only fly a short distance due to the card's resistance and alight again. Praise the puppy but lead it away to another pigeon several yards away. Don't train with carded birds without a check cord. The heavy card makes them easy to catch which you want to avoid at all costs.

The second method is the remote launcher. These have the advantage of allowing one to train alone without the help of an assistant. The disadvantage is the cost and the noise they make upon release. This sound can spook a sensitive puppy. Also, launcher's decrease the amount of scent just from their basic design. Despite these issues, remote launchers are a popular tool for training pointing. By the way, you will need at least two.

A Typical Day Afield

Your pup is on a 15' check cord with the JASA collar around his neck. There is a distinct breeze blowing. Two pigeons have been placed, either with a card or in a remote launcher. Walk the pup along, stopping several times for a few seconds to get the pup used to standing still while on the check cord. When you stop, give a light snap upwards with the JASA collar to instill the feel of the collar and say "Here". After a few seconds, give an "OK" verbal or a tap on the head to introduce the release command. Oddly, what you want to happen initially is for the bird to get up "wild" before the dog even points! Then, you can bring the pup to a stop again with just a "Here", as he watches the bird fly off a few yards. If the pup does stand and watch, lots of praise is in order. We are just trying to introduce the idea of standing still when birds fly at this point. It is easier for the pup to learn "Here", a command you have already introduced at this point. If this happens, turn and walk *away* from the area, again, stopping occasionally to instill this lesson. As you walk away, the pup is learning that it has to go with you...not after the bird. If you do this consistently, you will not have to deal later with the pup chasing after long gone birds or repointing birds they've seen alight miles away.

Keep working on the Stand Still/Here business as you gradually move to the next bird. You will be excited if he points the bird but, really, the pup can learn more from bumping the bird. Then, you can just stop him via the cord/JASA collar and watch the bird fly away. This is more of a teachable moment, as they say, than actually pointing the bird.

Continue this regime for five outings over two or three weeks. When you stop the pup, give it a "Here" command….no Whoa. By the end of these sessions, the pup will have learned that, if a bird flies, it is to Stand still and/or Come to You. Then, you can add your E-collar to the mix.

Keep the E-collar setting on a low level. You are transitioning from the JASA/check cord apparatus to the E-collar so we just want the pup to feel a low stimulation as a cue to Stand and Here. Begin using the E-collar with the same command "Here" at this point. See, "Here" serves the same purpose as "Whoa" long-term. A bird flushes and instead of chasing, the pup just comes to your side. At a test, you will be standing close to the dog so it actually won't move any and even if the dog comes to your side as the bird flies off, it has to be marked Steady. Besides, after really hunting the dog, the dog will usually not move to your side but just stand still instead. Using this system, the puppy is learning to come to you, stand still, release on cue, and love birds at the same time!

Now, you can begin using the E-collar in an interesting manner. With the dog, still on the check cord, walk it to an area where you've put the pigeons a few days before. The pup will be anticipating birds being there again but you stop him and give him the "Here" even though there is no bird scent around. This teaches the pup to be even more careful as it approaches bird cover. This is harmless because you are abiding by the rule: never "nick" the dog with birds on the ground! Once they fly, OK, but never, ever use E-collar stimulation with birds still on the ground. As a VR, I have failed dogs for "blinking" (turning away from birds and refusing to point them). This is invariably caused by overuse of the E-Collar and pressing that button with birds on the ground.

After this, you can walk to where a bird really is hidden. Once the bird flushes, try to use the JASA Collar/check cord tool plus the E-collar *at the same time.* It takes some quick hands but is very doable. Keep everything light. I used to try and turn the puppy a flip but that is totally unnecessary.

Things are progressing if the puppy begins to stop and stand still or come to you when a bird gets up wild or even if he bumps the bird. If he busts though a covey of quail but stops when they fly, you are a good dog trainer. This is all about stopping the chasing which is the first step toward true stanchness.

Eventually, you have to discard the collar/check cord and convert to just the E-collar. I start with a low setting to see how the pup reacts and gradually move to a higher setting searching for the "just right" level. If he stops and stands still, you are good to go. If this step fails, just go back to the JASA Collar/cord and re-teach the E-collar part. To train a truly finished dog around pointing, he has to learn the E-collar role.

Raise the bar over a few weeks by making things more challenging. I like to stop the dog and kick around in the brush as if I'm flushing a bird (which isn't even there). Ideally, they will just stand there but, let's be real, he's a puppy! If he has any drive at all, he want to jump in and help. Stay calm. Don't put on a show. Just gently place the dog a few inches back in a gentle manner. He will learn the lesson if you are patient.

Once you've accomplished this step, give him a real challenge. Same set-up, he's used to you faking a flush but this time, there's a bird there!! If he breaks on the flush, stop him with the E-collar. If he tries to come in on the bird before flush, just stop him with your hands and set him back without a verbal correction. If he is still, lots of praise is in order for the dog and you. The dog responds to the E-collar because you slowly taught the stopping with the JASA collar then moved to the E-collar. He isn't afraid of the nick because it's on a low setting and he's used to it and knows what he is supposed to do. Now, you have a rambunctious puppy. Will he break at times? Of course. Just stay the course. Be calm. Don't yell. Put him back to a standing position and keep trying. He will soon stand for a real flush just like he did with the fake one. You haven't said the word "Whoa" one time.

Over time, the flush of the bird becomes the cue to just stand still. How long will it take? Who knows? It just depends on you and your puppy but it will not be drudgery. If a dog will reliably stop to flush, is becomes much, much easier to attain true staunchness and steady to wing and shot. It is all about stopping on the flush.

Keep that E-collar setting as low as possible. We don't want a dog that dreads the flush! Signs of too much stimulation are tucking the tail, tacking his ears back, or certainly vocalizing. Most dogs respond to very light negative incentive if they know what is asked beforehand. Kennel the dog with no collar on it. Put the E-collar on the pup every time it is let out of its kennel. Place the E-collar on at the kennel gate with a bit of ceremony. The dog will learn to love that device because it means bird and fun.

Don't introduce retrieving at this point. Have your assistant bring a dead bird back to the puppy for now. This teaches him that even if he stands still, he will still get the bird in him mouth. Once you are sure he will stand still as the bird is shot, you can begin shooting a few for him all along.

Final Tips:

- Walk the dog with the JASA Collar/check cord around for a few minutes before approaching the birds.
- Stop several times and reinforce the "Here" command
- The pup should be willing to walk with you without pulling on the check cord all the time.
- Once he's settled in on the cord, work him crosswind of the bird; about 10 feet away
- If he points, don't stop, just walk into the flush promptly
- If he bolts for the bird, give him a little slack so he can bump the bird but not catch it!
- Once the bird flies, stop him and move away eventually heading to a second bird
- Between birds, stop and drill the stand still business
- We are really not trying to get the dog to point but just not to chase.
- Once he allows you to flush most of the birds, he knows what he is supposed to do
- When he does allow you to flush the bird (most of the time) you can begin setting him back (about a foot) and fake a flush with no bird present
- If the dog continues to "break", use the "spinning method": grab the free end of the JASA collar, lift the dog's front feet off the ground and gently spin him around one time. No whipping, no yelling, no other physical correction. Again, just move him back a few inches. If your puppy is "soft", just set the dog back—skip the spinning.
- Since your dog has been wearing the E-collar on all outings, it is used to its presence. Once it is stopping to flush with the JASA collar, begin using low settings and nick the pup along with the JASA collar pinch eventually moving over to only the E-collar.
- Never pinch the dog or nick him when birds are being scented or seen.
- It is fine to work on several birds after a few weeks but if he performs correctly, stop and put him up. Always quit on a good note.
- If you find a system that you like better, use it but don't mix systems. Get one and stay with it.
- While keeping the puppy on a check cord will decrease its search to a degree, for this stage, the check cord is essential. Trying to teach a young dog bird manners while running free is futile.

If you continue this regime and use birds that fly well, one or two birds per session, and things will begin to fall in place. Be patient. Impulsive, loud people don't make good dog trainers. Be sure and use good flying birds. Dizzied, tired, unhealthy birds can destroy your progress. If you cannot find wild pigeons, use the remote releasers. Don't try to get him to point every bird. Remember, he is learning just as much from wild flushed ones as the ones he points. After several weeks of this training system, put out some good flying quail or chukars and see what happens. Your puppy has deep genetic potential for pointing. Let it develop.

To teach real steadiness, rig up a wooden pallet that you beat someone out of, nail some boards on it or some plywood to give the pallet a uniform surface with no openings. Drive a metal stake down at one corner of the pallet and attach a chain to the stake; about 6 feet long. Make sure the stake is deep in the ground and the puppy cannot pull it out. On the far end of the chain rig a strong snap to which you can attach your JASA collar.

Place the dog on the pallet, give it a "Sit" and place the JASA collar, attached to the chain, on his neck. Take one of your pigeons and toss it about 15 feet out in front of the pup. Doubtlessly, he will bolt to catch it and just as he reaches the end of the chain/collar apparatus, quietly say "Whoa". He will hit the end but stop quickly due to the JASA collar. Over a day or two, the pup will begin to just sit on the pallet while you move the pigeon closer and closer and even wave the live bird in front of his muzzle. You can transfer the word "Whoa" to E-collar correction and eventually the lesson will transfer to the field.

In addition, you can build a Pigeon Pole for a very few dollars. Take a long piece of ¾" PVC pipe, about 10 feet long. On one end, glue a cap in which you have drilled a hole and placed a small eye bolt with a nut inside. The eye bolt should rotate freely. Tie a long (12 feet) piece of soft twine to the eyebolt. Then, find a 3 foot piece of rebar, drive it into the ground about a foot before placing the open end of the long PVC pipe over it. It will tilt a little but will be semi-flexible. Using a pigeon, tie the end of the soft twine to both its legs and toss it on the ground about 8 feet from the base of the pole. This set-up should be in your yard or some other clean area.

Bring your pup around a corner, on a check cord, and advance toward the bird. Hopefully, the pup will stop and point! If it charges the bird, using your check cord/JASA collar, stop him but not brutally. We don't want this to be a negative experience. Just be patient and quiet. Don't say anything at this point unless you've completed the Whoa training on the pallet mentioned above. A gentle "Whoa" is OK but no yelling. Have an assistant pick the bird up and toss it to fly around the pole but make sure the bird can't land on or near your puppy. Lead the pup off and repeat this drill again. Continue over several days until the pup totally understands that he isn't to try and catch the bird. I want to stress that we don't want a lot of jerking, harsh yelling or punishment during the Pigeon Pole drills. Keep it fun. The puppy must learn to love birds.

"It's all About Whoa."—one of my bird dog training buddies

If you think about Pointing in the broadest sense, it just means standing still when they smell a bird. That's it. Oh, we like a stylish, intense point but if the dog just stops and stands there, you can kill a lot of birds with it. Well, how do you get that to happen?

I hate to simplify it too much, but is really is all about "Whoa". Here's how I do it. Beginning as a little puppy, say 16 weeks, I begin using the word "Whoa" as often as I can. Before the puppy comes out of its crate or kennel; before it comes through a door, before it jumps in the kennel; time after time….and stop the puppy with your hand to teach it what you want.

Eventually, it will understand the term. Then, advance to the puppy merely standing (or sitting) on lead while you step five or six feet away. If the puppy is treat-driven (most are) step back to it and give it a treat. Work on this daily as you play with or train the puppy. Over time, you will be able to say "Whoa" when the pup is 20-30 yards away and it will stop and/or sit. This is without boards, barrels, ropes, stakes etc. It just requires that you begin very early.

By the time the pup is hunting for birds, it will know the word "Whoa". This makes the whole "breaking" of the dog much, much easier. Sure, you will no doubt have to use the electronic collar to reinforce the command (but never using it with the birds on the ground!) or at least a check cord. But, if the command has been instilled over months, the whole process will go much more smoothly.

Chapter Seven: Retrieving

"Most of the failures at JGHV tests involve some form of a failed retrieve."

--an experienced judge

"Waving a hat and yelling Good Boy has replaced solid Force Fetching"

--a judge at a recent test

Just what are we looking for in a versatile dog's retrieving work? I mean, really, what do we have to have? There are four things:

- Good "mouth"; no chewing, biting or damaging of edible game
- A dog that will retrieve, even with tempting distractions
- A fast, enthusiastic retriever with "style"
- Once trained, maintaining those lessons for life

So, how do we get to this point? While there may be dogs that accomplish this level naturally, most don't. Would it be better if we developed dogs that had these characteristics via breeding? Certainly. But, with the myriad of skills that a finished versatile dog must possess, breeding for the natural tendency to deliver to hand with minimal training would have to come with loss of other required genetics. So, we are left with the only viable option: The Forced Retrieve.

While the training process should be called the Conditioned Retrieve, the Forced Retrieve term and its synonym, the Force Fetch process is a more used term, which is the term to be used in this book, The Force Fetch or FF for short.

FF'ing a dog is a daunting process. It takes lots of time, patience, and skill to work. Let's learn about it.

The "Forced Retrieve":[3]

First, let's get this out of the way: Most versatile pups will retrieve and retrieve and retrieve anything you will throw for them from sticks to tennis balls to training dummies and Dokken® ducks just because they are genetically disposed to do it. In fact, 90% of the time, they will retrieve as long as you will throw something. But, that is 90%. There is that 10% of the time they will either refuse or not complete the retrieve (usually at a test). That is why we "force" them to perform. We want 100%. All dogs do two things "naturally": they use their nose to detect scent and they chase stuff. Everything else we ask them to do is a trained/conditioned response to teaching and repetition. For example, take a well-bred pup and just turn him loose for three years with no training sessions. Then, take him out and throw a dummy for him and see how well he retrieves. He won't.

The term "force" is a bad one because it conjures images of harsh punishment which is absolutely not an accurate picture. A better term is the "conditioned retrieve" but that term has just never caught on, so we continue to use the force retrieve as a designation. For the purposes of this book, we will use the term "Forced Fetch" or FF to explain the rationale and methodology.

No one wants a sulking, reluctant retriever. Harsh and abusive methods will not work. As the old saying goes "A properly forced dog should not look forced."

The correct FF consists of many steps and lessons: Hold, Fetch, Collar Conditioned to Fetch, Walking Fetch, and Forcing to a Pile (of dummies), sitting for delivery either at side or in front, and Water Forcing to the far side of the pond.

Before the FF process begins, the dog should be obedient. That means they will come to you, sit on command, and walk at heel in a calm manner. Up to this point, we have been using passive "suggestive" training to get the puppy to comply. Prior to serious FF beginning, the ante needs to go up. The three important commands that FF requires are Here, Heel, and Sit.

Strict "Here"

Assuming your dog is coming when called due to your passive training using petting and/or treats when the pup arrives, you should begin insisting on a prompt recall when the "Here" command is given.

Use a long rope at first for maximum control and your e-collar set on the lowest setting, say "Here" and press the continuous button until the dog arrives at your side. The only way it can turn off the stimulation is to come to your side. If the puppy is compliant already around this command, it can just be re-enforced by giving the "Here" command and continuous stimulation as the dog comes to you without the use of the rope. Several repetitions or this tactic will result in a dog that runs as fast as possible to you upon the "Here" command.

Strict "Sit" and Strict "Heel"

Dogs prefer not to be precise. But, requiring a perfect "Sit" sets the stage for all upcoming work around FF'ing as we will require precise compliance. Thus, the strict "Sit" teaches the dog that we won't give an inch on anything and leads to a dog that scores well at any test and, more importantly, becomes a truly finished hunting dog. The ideal tool for teaching the strict "Sit" is the Heeling Stick. The stick, once again, is not for whipping the dog but to instill a rapid, sharp sit on one command. This means a "tap" not a painful whack. They'll get the message.

During the passive training stage of "Sit", you said "Sit" and probably pressed down on the hindquarters and pulled straight up on the choke chain collar/leash. During that time, practically any type of sitting posture was OK; you were just glad the dog would sit! Now, we want a more precise execution. That means with both rear legs up under the dog as opposed to sitting sideways on one haunch. Early in the use of the Heeling Stick, dogs tend to sit to one side because they are not yet conditioned to the tap with the stick. Also, he may just try to get away from you. You must be persistent because not only are you teaching the correct sit posture, you are conditioning the dog to pressure or correction (and turning it off). A dog that is used to this type training is a much more focused and easily trained dog. If he sits to one side, just use your foot to put mild pressure on the incorrect toe of the dog. Don't just stand still during this process. Move away from the dog or nudge him with your knee if he's too close or step forward and help him move closer to you if he's too far out. Be calm and consistent until he can repeat the process reliably.

The simple Heeling Stick is one of the most valuable training tools available. But, many are confused as to its daily use. First, it should be carried correctly. Most experts recommend it should be held in the hand on the same side as the dog with the handle in your palm and the business end up against your shoulder. Grip it like an umbrella over your shoulder. If you keep it in the other hand, you have to come across your body with a sweeping motion that just causes a dog to shy away from it. Don't carry it pointed to the ground either. This requires you to bring the stick up before providing correction. As with all negative feedback, timing is crucial. You want the stick where it can be applied instantly. Another option is to carry it in the opposite hand and apply the tap behind your back. This hides the stick from the dog's view and alleviates the dog avoiding it or becoming shy of it. Of course, carrying it in your back pocket is worthless.

You want the correction for "Sit" to be straight down so the dog sees minimal motion as the tap is applied. If your dog yelps when you correct him, you are hitting him too hard!

Using the Heeling Stick, you can teach the strict "Sit" and strict "Heeling". Assuming the dog is walking comfortably on lead with or without a choke chain or JASA collar, heeling off lead will be straightforward. While somewhat counter-intuitive, if the dog fails to Heel correctly on one command, the tap should be on his hindquarters just like on the "Sit" command. He is conditioned to the tap on his hindquarters as a correction for poor performance.

While starting, straight line Heeling is fine, you should move quickly to figure-eights and other variations. Also, vary your speed from a slow walk to jogging. This helps the dog remain focused and the varying speed is a typical requirement by VGP judges.

Some dogs get so involved in the Sit command they become reluctant to get up and follow you when you say Heel. This is called "lagging" and is actually a good sign that the dog comprehends the Sit command. If this happens, just clap your hands or become more animated when you say Heel and the dog will get over his reluctance.

Eventually, you want to walk the dog at Heel, say Sit, and continue walking without breaking stride. The dog needs to remain sitting until you say Heel again. The vast majority of dogs will require correction at this stage. Again, try not to use the word Stay. Sit implies staying.

After each tense session around these forced training regimes, one should end with on a happy note. For example, say you've been Heeling and Sitting for several days and the dog is obviously getting the hang of it. You've made a few corrections lately but overall, the dog is complying almost every time. This is the time to introduce the powerful phrase "Good girl" or "Good boy". Initially, just say the words in a normal voice but gradually add some more enthusiasm and joy in your voice. If you go too quickly to the enthusiastic version, the dog may "break" and jump for joy himself. He needs to learn, however, to be happy and make his owner happy and remain obedient at the same time. Then, throw some short bumper retrieves for him just for fun or at the least give him a great petting session.

Months later, when you are at a test or in a difficult hunting situation, that simple phrase "Good boy" or "Good girl" can work magic in calming the dog and getting it refocused. Don't overuse the phrase and keep it just for finishing a tough training session.

When these three crucial training commands are mastered, you can move on to the actual FF process. It is much, much easier to FF an obedient dog.

The Actual Force Fetch Process

[*The FF method outlined here is essentially the same as Graham Evan's method outlined in his excellent book SmartFetch. For more detailed information, it is strongly suggested that one actually purchase Mr. Evan's book. It is well worth the investment however, as of this date, the book is out of print.-the author*]

There is a general argument among owners and trainers around continuing field and water work while FF is going on. Every dog is different, but, as a general rule, we suspend other training until FF is completed. One simple reason is that you probably won't have much extra time if you give the FF a good effort. That is enough hassle for most of us. Another controversy exists around the best age to begin FF. With many retriever breeds (and in the hands of many retriever trainers), FF can begin as soon as the puppy has its adult teeth, i.e. about six months of age. In my experience, versatile pups thrive better during the FF process if it begins after the VJP test in the spring. I like to take a short break after that test, relax and let the dog relax for two or three weeks, then begin the FF process. One has plenty of time to complete this training and get the dog into drills for blind retrieves, drags, etc. over the summer in preparation for the HZP in the fall. While dogs vary a lot, many versatile pups are just not mentally ready for the pressure of FF at an earlier age. Some of this depends on their birth date. For example, a puppy born in early November will be six months old in May. They don't test in the VJP until the following spring so there is not a lot to do with them during the summer, so FF might be OK for this age dog. If a puppy is born in January or February, by the time it is six-eight months old, one needs to be focused on VJP preparation and FF training will interfere with exposure to birds, searching, and tracking training. In the final analysis, the decision around timing is up to the individual owner/trainer.

The first step in FF is the "Hold" command. We all see dogs bringing the rabbit or duck back after a drag holding it like a cigar; by either end. A proper hold is in the middle of the object's body. This goes back to the first part of FF. One can use many different objects as they start the FF process: a simple dowel, small bumper (not recommended), or the best: a new, small paint roller. Dogs don't mind them as much because they are soft and light and about the right size.

Since you have required the strict Sit command, you will have an easier time of FF. Approach FF with a calm, methodical mindset. Go easy.

Place the object in his mouth and say "Hold". Be sure the dog's lips are not impinged on the object to avoid pain and get the object behind the upper and lower canine teeth. If he holds it, repeat the command several times as you pet him and make sweet-talk to him. Initially, you can be patient if he spits it out but you must move on to a more insistent tone. Tapping him on the chin or pressing in the "V" between the lower jaws will help him refrain from dropping the object.

Unlike most other commands, both Fetch and Hold are strictly forced. It is difficult to train these steps in a passive manner so this is a totally new process for the dog. As a result, continual consistency and strict enforcement are fundamental here.

Once the dog is holding reliably, it is time to "proof" his Hold. Simply make false reaches for the object (but don't take it), tap the ends of the object to dare him to release it. If he drops it, you must correct him at that time. Keep in mind, so far we have not started the ear pinch so if he drops the object, you will just have to correct him verbally or with a tap on the chin.

After he has passed the proofing stage, you should begin Heeling while Holding. Take it slow and walk in a short, straight line at first with him holding the object. Then, graduate to circles, figure eights, squares, etc. all with him holding the object without dropping it. Once he's proven that he will hold the object while walking at your side, you can move to the dreaded Fetch command.

There are a number of ways to accomplish the Fetch command and forcing the dog to comply. You should study several methods and find one that you are comfortable with but do not mix the various systems. Pick one and stick with it.

This method is one that has worked for me. However, you must attend to each detail of this method for success. There are no real short-cuts. Again, I am assuming your dog is totally reliable on Sit, Here, and Heel. There may be lapses during the FF and you will have to go back and freshen the dog's training around these tasks but, overall, he should be solid on those commands. The caveat is to refrain from tweaking those commands as you attempt the FF. To try and refresh Sit while you are FF'ing can confuse the dog.

Pick a quiet area, even inside your shop or garage, where there are few distractions. At the least, go somewhere in the yard that is quiet and a bit isolated. Take a fresh, new paint roller with you. I recommend that you don't switch objects early on. Some trainers like to show off their dog's FF ability by asking it to retrieve everything from a WD-40® can to a hairbrush. In my view, this is not necessary or recommended. As the dog progresses, it is fine to progress to a small training dummy but not at first. You don't want to fight your battles with something the dog is supposed to enjoy retrieving.

One question that needs to be answered initially is "To Table or Not to Table?" Most of us started with a "forcing table" in our first efforts but since you will be doing the FF training on the ground within a few days, the table is probably superfluous. Note that the long tables with cables and uprights and pulleys are designed for the toe hitch method using a string on the dog's foot. Since I recommend the ear pinch method, these complex tables are of minimal value. A simple table about 12 inches off the ground with an upright back side can be made out of one piece of plywood and one two-by-four will suffice for FF the DD pup or, no table at all is fine too. If the dog resists, just stand next to your house or a wall for restraint.

Place an e-collar on the dog and walk the dog calmly to the designated area keeping obedience commands to a minimum. Give the dog a "Sit" command. Sit down in a chair next to the dog. Loop three fingers under his collar to help control the dog. Using your thumb and forefinger, place the dog's ear flap over the collar buckle. This same exact routine must be used during each session. Do not let go of the ear. The only thing the dog has to realize and grasp is whether or not you are applying pressure to the ear. Everything else remains constant. Keep in mind, the dog has no idea how to turn off the negative feedback at this time so patience and fairness is in order. See, in other tasks like sitting and heeling, we initiated the training with passive "showing him how to do it' first then advanced to strict, forced compliance. Here, we are going straight to the forcing method of teaching. There is the rub.

Since the dog has been passively trained to Hold, you can anticipate that he will in fact hold the object once it is in his mouth.

Using fairly light pressure at first, press the ear against the buckle and say "Fetch". Begin pressure at the first sound of the "F" in fetch and place the object in his mouth. If he holds it, pet his head but don't say anything. Some dogs will resist and yelp while others almost fail to notice the pressure. All we are really interested in is "Does the dog feel the pressure and want to turn it off?" Every dog is different and some dogs will respond by simply sitting there and clamping their mouth shut while others will howl at the slightest pressure. Begin and maintain low to moderate pressure until you are certain the dog requires more pressure. This decision will be made over a few days and many repetitions at moderate pressure. You might be surprised at how the dog responds to fairly low pressure if you are patient.

Initially, you will probably have to place the roller in the dog's mouth but shortly it will figure out that when the object goes in his mouth, the pinch goes away. Keep your praise minimal but petting his head is fine. Do everything the same way every time and just keep trying.

Shortly (or not), the dog will understand the game and begin reaching for the object. At first, hold it close to his mouth so he can be successful at turning off the pressure. Then, gradually, hold it a little farther out so he has to work to stop the pressure. As the dog progresses, there is temptation to "see if he'll do it without the pressure". Do not fall into that trap. The wheels can come off if you try that at this stage! The FF process takes time; lots of it. You are "conditioning" the dog and conditioning by definition requires time and repetition.

Once you are totally satisfied that he understands that the only way he can turn the pressure off is by taking the roller in his mouth, e.g. consistently reaches for the object at the first sign of pressure and the first sound of the "F" in fetch, you can assume you are making progress. Don't worry if the dog yelps or does not yelp. The key is in his eyes.

Once the dog is reaching several inches to grab the object, you should begin requiring him to take a step towards it. Just one step at first is sufficient. Gradually, you can begin taking a step yourself to make the distance a foot or two away from the dog's mouth. Remember, we are applying pressure each and every time at this point. Think "baby steps" in this whole process.

A common question we hear is "How long will it take?" but, frankly, there is no answer that applies to every dog. In my experience, DD's are fairly easy to FF but that can backfire on you. You begin to think the dog is totally FF'd when, actually, it needs more conditioning. I have seen dogs that take eight weeks before they begin to reach for the object but then become very compliant and dependable afterwards.

When the dog is reliably reaching for the object and you think you are making real progress, you should restrain the dog to insure the dog is, in fact, becoming FF'd. Simply begin the

FF session as usual with a few reaches then hold back on the collar a bit to make the dog work a bit to make the grab. If the dog overcomes this restraint and insists on getting the roller, you are doing fine but if he simply stops reaching just because you've held back on the collar, you still need conditioning. This can be accomplished by increasing the pressure on the ear because the dog understands what is required but keep the restraint level (holding the dog back) about the same. The key here is that you must be able to stop the dog from reaching for the object with some level of restraint which is somewhat confusing. Holding the dog back from the object and applying more and more pinch-pressure will insure success long-term. Don't just hold the dog back totally but let him pull toward the object requiring more and more effort on his (and your) part. You want a dog that wants that object no matter what it takes. Once you are confident, you can give him two or three grabs without restraint (but still with ear pinch) with praise as a reward.

Once you have progressed past the reaching stage with restraint, you should begin using a small, plastic training dummy as you transition to more advanced FF steps. At this stage, you should begin transitioning to the ground for his FF training. It is important that you still hold the object in your hand as you place it on the ground in front of the dog. For many dogs, picking the object up off the ground is a giant step to take and keeping the object in your hand is just one way of making the evolution easier. Begin by holding the object below his muzzle and gradually extend the distance until it is actually touching the ground. Remember, we are talking baby steps. Early on, just tilt the dummy down so he doesn't have to grab it directly off the floor or ground. It is nice to have a short rope on the dummy. As you progress you can move your hand to the end of the rope to help ensure success during this transition. Going to the ground is typically the biggest hurdle we face in FF.

By this time, the dog should show great determination to get the dummy but you should still be holding the collar and applying pressure. If this is happening, you can move to the Walking Fetch. Simply lay a row of dummies in a straight line and heel your dog along that line. Stopping at each bumper, say "Fetch", pinch the ear, after he picks it up, say "Hold" (which you can delete after a few repetitions), "Heel", "Sit" and "Give" or "Drop" as he releases the object. Again, if the dog refuses for some reason, re-enforce with pressure. This process can be a strain on your back but is absolutely necessary.

I need to include a few words about "stick fetching" which simply means the use of the Heeling Stick to force the dog to fetch. This tool has been used by many, many trainers and can be of value. However, if the groundwork has been laid in the initial FF training, the stick method is probably not necessary. Typically, I don't take the time to stick fetch because I am under pressure to the get the dog ready for the HZP and need to move on to the next step: FF with the electronic collar.

Electronic training collars used to be controversial. That was before we learned some important facts about them: they don't "teach" anything; they require great discretion in their use, and they are just another tool to help with training. Since we have learned about the two methods of teaching a dog, passive and forced, the electronic collar is a tool for *forcing* compliance; nothing more and nothing less.

The term "collar conditioning" was covered previously but is still somewhat confusing to new trainers but it just comes down to teaching the dog that the new negative pressure comes from his trainer via the collar stimulation. To help with this, after using the Bark Collar, I tie previous negative feedback to which the dog is accustomed to the new collar stimulation. For example, when we were teaching the strict Sit, we used the Heeling Stick to provide correction. Now, we will simply use the same stick along with the collar stimulation to educate our pupil on the connection between the two and begin the transition to pure collar training.

Here is a supplemental format for collar conditioning a dog around Heel and Sit: While walking in a straight line, give the dog a Sit, tap it with the stick two or three times to get things in perspective then give a Sit command along with the stick tap plus a "nick" with the collar on a very low setting. [Note: Generally, we don't use the nick button very often. Ideally, one would use the Continuous button again at a very low setting and release it when the dog sits. But, most dogs sit quickly at this point so it may be difficult to use the Continuous button in a timely fashion. As a result, a Nick here might be easier and teach the dog without error.] While we want to be cautious, it is good to increase the level of stimulation until the dog's reaction shows that we are getting it too hot. For Tritronics collars, a level of 2 or 3 should be enough where a Dogtra should be around 20-30.

Once the dog is responding to the collar stimulation for Sit, move on to Heeling but as a separate exercise. While practicing Heeling with the collar, don't use it to force Sit (go back to the stick if correction is required) but do use the collar as you give the Heel command. This lesson is merely to acquaint the dog with the collar stimulation around another command.

Now, we are ready to force the fetch command with the collar. The dog has been "collar conditioned". Begin by repeating the FF with the ear pinch to get things going in the correct manner. Even if the dog is readily reaching and grabbing the dummy, pinch the ear. Then, while still pinching the ear, apply low but continuous collar stimulation while holding the object directly in front of the dog's muzzle to help insure compliance quickly. After reaching a level of collar stimulation that approaches the maximum for your individual dog, begin backing down on the collar setting until you are getting a quick response at the lowest level possible. Once this correct level is established, go through the same steps you did with the ear pinch: hold the object in front of the dog, then work it down to the ground over a day or two then on to the Walking Fetch as previously described. Always go back to the ear pinch if the dog seems confused or refuses. Your goal is to gradually back off the level of stimulation until it is not required. Keep in mind; you will be using the collar for months in training as opposed to the ear pinch so it is not necessary to drill him over and over once the dog has gotten the idea of the collar stimulation equals Fetch. That will be solidified in daily training from now on.

Introduction of the new command "Back" for blind retrieving should be instituted at this time. The word "Fetch" is a "hot" word and should only be used in the future if the dog drops the object or creates some other horrendous mistake. "Back" will be the standard command for making all the retrieves at a JGHV test. To introduce this command, just put a small (three) pile of dummies about 20 yards away. Send him with low level e-collar stimulation all the way to the pile which should be easy at this point. Once he picks up the dummy, stop the stimulation and bring him back to you using a long check cord. By this time, he will be so fired up about going to the pile, he will respond to anything you say. Give him a "Back", stimulate with the collar on low setting again and watch him go to the pile. To make things easier, you can alternate "Fetch" with "Back" for a few days until the transition to the "Back" command is complete. Some trainers wait until they are doing "marked" retrieves, i.e. throwing a dummy, to introduce the "Back" command. By this time, the dog should reliably go to the pile of dummies every time and bring one back. If this is occurring, follow the steps used previously by gradually backing off the stimulation level until you can send him without stimulation and he will perform 100% of the time.

Now, for a few extra tips:

You need to learn to hold the dummy and the e-collar transmitter in the same hand. At first, it may be awkward but with practice, anyone can do it. Just hold the transmitter along with the dummy out in front of the dog's muzzle with your finger on the button as you also hold the dummy's end with the rope hole on it between two fingers (and the other hand is on the collar). Initially, you will need to be able to apply ear pressure, collar pressure and manage the dummy position all at one time. It takes some practice but is doable.

If the dog is hesitant to "Give" or "Drop" just roll the lower lip up over the lower incisor teeth and press and he'll give it up.

If the dog has a bad hold on the object, adjust the position of the item with an ear pinch too and later with e-collar stimulation.

As you prepare for the various tests, you should FF your dog on the game animals it will be required to retrieve: rabbits, ducks, and either a raccoon or fox. Using a thawed animal, simply repeat the steps used on the dummies with each individual animal. Yes, ear pinch and collar stimulation should be included for maximum performance at the tests.

Don't forget to work on Manner of Retrieve during your drills. Correct your dog for parading around with the dummy, sitting too far from you, etc. Sloppy Manner of Retrieve can cost you points during testing.

A German trainer was asked once "How can I tell when my dog is totally Force Fetched". His answer was "When he completed 1000 retrieves without fail." Of course, this includes all the rabbit and duck drags, all the water retrieves and all the retrieves on dummies during training. It doesn't take long for them to add up.

Begin the classic "forcing to a pile" which really does not mean a pile of dummies but typically nine of them laid like 9-ball on a pool table, e.g. in a diamond shape with about 2 feet between the dummies. Gradually stretch the distance farther and farther until you've gotten at least 100 yards. Now, you can start real training.

Blind Retrieves

For me, this has been the most challenging task to teach a young dog. There's nothing in the dog's genetic makeup to drive swimming across some water to an object they haven't seen splash and have no idea is even there. The Blind Retrieve also provides the basis for the Search Behind a Live Duck and the Search Without a Duck at the VGP. The pup learns that if you send it, there's something out there even on the far shore of a large pond.

I like to start with a visual aid in the yard. I like a five-gallon white bucket. Simply put the bucket a short distance away, say 30 yards. Walk your dog up to it and let the pup see you drop 3 dummies by the bucket. Walk back and tell the dog "Dead Bird". When he looks at the bucket, say "Good" and quickly say "Back". He should be able to see the dummies so will promptly run and get one. Send him back for the other two using the same format. Gradually, over several days, move the bucket further and further until the pup will go 100 yards to the bucket. Make sure the area is short-cropped, no cover so he can actually see the bucket. After a week or so, repeat the drill two times then, put the bucket up and just put the dummies in the same place. Hopefully, he will remember about where they were and find them for you. A good way to speed the process is to start a short distance away and as the pup goes for a dummy, walk away from the bucket making the pup go further and further each time. Putting five or six dummies near the aid allows you to eventually be 50-75 yards away on the last few objects.

After the pup is solid on this drill and no longer needs the bucket in the yard, it is time to move to water. The first elementary drill is a simple one: with the pup in the truck, toss a large white dummy about 20 yards out in some still water. Lead the pup to the bank where he can see the dummy and send him for it. Now, for the first time, he's retrieved an object in the water that he did not see splash. We are on the way. I'd repeat this 2-3 times but you have to move on to the real stuff.

Place the good old bucket on the far shore of a small pond...20-30 yards away. After placing a dummy or two in the edge of the water near the bucket, bring your puppy to the edge of the near water and using the mantra "Dead Bird"...he sees the bucket, say "Good" and then "Back". The "Dead Bird" assures the dog that it is a Blind Retrieve. "Good" teaches him to look in the correct direction, and "Back" of course sends him. Overtime, without the bucket to attract him, the "Good" isn't given until he looks at the location of the duck/dummy. It will take a while but if you continue to drill this word, he will learn that he will only be sent when he's looking in the right direction.

After several drills with the bucket, remove it. Again, we are looking for fairly short retrieves at this point. We want him to learn the "Good" command and that the duck is always on the far side of the water whether is 15 yards or 100 yards. Gradually begin extending the distance until after a month, he will swim 50 yards or more to the area of the duck.

This is a good time to use the Retrieve-R-Trainer. Yes, you can use marked falls at first. Typically, I will fire one dummy off while the dog is in the truck and cannot see or hear the splash way out there. Then, with the pup at your side, fire the marked one that he sees hit. Send him out and he will pick up one of them. Then, after the return, try him without a shot to see if he will swim out the area and find the first one you shot. This teaches l-o-n-g retrieves which, incidentally, drives long searches for ducks at the HZP and VGP tests. He learns that the duck can be a long way off.

A common problem is the dog that swims out a few yards and starts circling. This usually comes from the trainer throwing too many dummies for the pup to retrieve that he sees hit and aren't far away. But, some dogs just don't get it that they need to go further to find the duck. This is a good time to use the E-Collar. After he's done a lot of blinds and you've pointed to the far shore with your extended arm reassuring him with more "Back" commands, if he starts to veer to an island, into the wind (common) or even comes back to the near shore, you can give him a low stimulation with the collar and a "A-h-n-n-n-t". If he's been truly FF'd, he will get the message. Some trainers, "force" the dog all the way across the water using the collar at a low setting they keep the stimulation up until the dog finds the duck or at least gets to the far bank. The only way the dog can turn the electricity off is to go to the far bank. I have done this with some dogs and, yes, it works. But, you don't want the dog to dread this work and be looking back at you with a worried look on his face while swimming across. So, it is OK to do but try to teach the subject without it at first. This step is for the difficult case.

Live duck searches need to be instituted after the pup has the Blind down fairly well. Of course, this begins training for the Search subject but also drives desire to do the Blinds too.

THE TESTS

Chapter Eight: The VJP

For the new handler, this will usually be their first experience at a JGHV test. If their breeder has been an active participant and if one has been to training days, read a bunch of written information, and has the Rule Book, the VZPO memorized, things should go well. There is, however, a misconception on some handler's parts that since this is a "natural ability" test, little preparation is required. Well, that is true if you don't want to score well. But, if you want to give your puppy the best opportunity to excel, then certainly training is important. Now, it is somewhat difficult to actually fail this spring test. Gun shyness, blinking (fear of birds), or inability to catch the puppy are the three main reasons for a VJP failure. Otherwise, we just need to try and get a good score which is generally considered anything over 65 VJP points.

There are, essentially three subjects at this test: Searching, Pointing, and the Rabbit Track. Let's take a closer look at how the day will go:

Arrival: You will have received a "Program" for the test outlining when you actually test, who you will be testing with and who your judges (called VR's) will be. Be sure and arrive early. If possible, let your dog out away from the test area to "air out" a bit but always be at the test headquarters at the prescribed time per the Program. You will then present your Ahnentafel and a current Rabies vaccination certificate to the Test Director whose name will be listed on the Program. Some Test Directors will want to see your current hunting license too.

You will stand around a while as the judges gather and get their paperwork in order. The judges will have a short, private meeting with each other to discuss the format for the day, location of the various tasks, and generally commensurate about the test. Eventually, the Test Director will get everyone's attention and gather folks around for some introductions, welcoming, and encouragement. Finally, your Senior Judge will ask his or her group to join the judges for even more encouragement and some details about the test which will begin shortly. In due course, you and your dog along with the other handlers will follow the judges to the field to begin. It is fine to either have your dog on leash during these preliminaries or in the truck but it should be handy because you are going afield shortly. Often, prior to departing, the VR's will examine the tattoo number in the dog's right ear to insure you have presented the correct dog.

Let's say they elect to do Search first. The handler listed as "Dog 1" in the Program will go first and join the judges on the edge of a field. You will be asked to "take them hunting" which is essentially what you will be doing. After your dog has gotten into the Search and is comfortable, you or one of the judges will fire a 12-guage blank round to observe for gun sensitivity. A few minutes will pass and the shot will be repeated. Assuming your dog is comfortable with gunfire, you are being evaluated for Search from then on. Try to keep your vocal commands and whistle blasts to a minimum. The judges are looking for dogs that are Cooperative which isn't the same as Obedient. If you keep hacking on that whistle, sure your dog will come around but that's Obedient. The judges are looking for a dog that checks with its handler, kinda keeps an eye on the handler, etc. without any commands. But, don't be afraid to give a tweet on your whistle when needed; just be conservative with its use. How does one get a high Search score? Well, a methodical, windshield-wiper pattern is impressive. The actual range is not crucial but certainly a pup should plunge into likely game cover and stay out front a lot. Running back and forth in a vertical pattern is not as effective in finding game as the side-to-side pattern. Now, dogs that Search primarily at a trot will not score well. The Search evaluation will continue for several minutes and, often, end in a "bird field" where pointing will be evaluated. If your dog is plodder, you can walk fast to encourage the dog to expand its search. If your dog is often a dot on the horizon, you might potter along yourself in hopes the pup will stay in sight. You can walk in a zig-zag pattern to encourage a good search too. To whistle or not? Well, as I said, ideally, tweeting on the thing is kept to a minimum. But, certainly, if you get uncomfortable with the dog's far out range, a short blast or two is OK. What VR's generally don't like is the dog that hunts for itself with no concern or idea where its handler is. These dogs often make great hunting dogs as they mature but will need to learn to hunt with the handler more.

To get a high score in the Search subject, one needs to take their puppy on lots of trips afield. Now, to just let a puppy run and run, while acceptable, to really establish a great searching dog, it needs to find game on a regular basis. See, the standard calls for a "will to find". So, the puppy needs to learn to find something during its outings. This drives that "will". Typically, this means planted birds; either pigeons or better, good flying quail, pheasants, chukkars, etc. This teaches the dog that there is something out there...not just butterflies and mice. During these practice runs, if the puppy is searching and getting pretty far away, let it go. Generally, you want to expand the search at this point because lots of puppies are bonded with you and want to hang around your area. True enough, to find game and kill it, a dog ranging at 50-75 yards is often most effective but, at this point, you want the puppy on the edge of its search range. You can decrease that range later if needed.

As the Search subject in concluded, usually you and your dog will be approaching an area where upland birds are known to be. The VR's will be evaluating Pointing at this time. To score well at the VJP, your pup just needs to show that it has the natural, inherited trait to point game. A long, staunch point is not required. But, a flash point and bumping is not the way to score high either. So, some training for the subject is certainly in order. If you've worked with the pointing training outlined in earlier chapters you should be fine. But, there are some tactics that will help your pup during this test too. For example, check the wind! Try to handle the pup downwind of the birds. VR's see it all the time: a handler just wanders willy-nilly toward the ostensible birds and the pup bumps one or two because it closes on the bird from the up wind side. Once the puppy flushes a bird, it is more difficult to get a nice point because the pup is in the "catch it" mode. Try to avoid this situation by handling the dog downwind.

If the pup stops and stands still when it smells the bird, you stop too. The judges will tell you, in a minute or two, to "Get Your Dog". Approach from the front of the dog if possible and just try to get your hands on it. If the bird flushes and the puppy chases it off, there is no penalty at this test but, realistically, you gotta catch him at some point. So, now, you can get on that whistle, call the dog, whatever it takes to get it back promptly. VR's see dogs that run for two hundred yards after a bird and take forever to apprehend. Again, this won't affect the score but it can delay the test. I have seen dogs that could not be caught at a VJP and this can result in failure.

The last subject is the all-important Rabbit Track. This subject is crucial because it is a multiplier of "2" in your score. The format typically goes like this: the handlers will be leading their puppies as a loose group in an area where rabbits abound (hopefully). Typically, no choke chain collars are allowed so teaching your dog to Heel helps make for a easier time of the waiting period. At some point, a VR will yell "Rabbit...Rabbit" and Dog 1 will quickly advance to the area. The judge will show the handler where the rabbit was jumped or at least first seen and the pup will be asked to track the scent line. The rules say that the VR's must actually see the rabbit and the handler/dog team should not see it. They are looking for scent tracking; not a sight chase. Eventually, all the dogs in the group will be given several opportunities to track a rabbit and the judges will arrive at a score for this subject. Since this is an important part of the test, let's take a closer look at it.

Training for this subject comes down to two components: Exposure to rabbit tracks and the Release of the Dog on the Track. Exposure can be done in two ways: Rabbit Drags with a dead rabbit or actual tracking of live rabbits. By far, the best approach is the live rabbit. To accomplish this you have to have, well, a lot of rabbits. First, find a landowner that has a lot of rabbits and get permission to ride around late in the day or at night and "shine" for rabbits. This is the method that has worked best for me. The pup is in the front seat with an e-collar on and a leash attached. You ride down a field road and see a rabbit. Keep your eye on the bunny as it hops off and mark the exact place it entered cover. Get the puppy out, on leash, and walk to the area. Say "Track It; Track It" over and over. If you have exposed the puppy to this command on treat tracks as a youngster, it will know to put its head down and will smell the game's scent. Repeating this exercise two or three times per week for a month before the VJP test will help insure a high score on this subject.

A less desirable option is dragging a dead rabbit as a substitute tracking objective. While this is good, it is no substitute for the real thing. But, it does get the puppy and you practice around getting the dog off on the track which is the second component.

There are several ways to smoothly release your puppy on the rabbit track but it all comes down to a "slip" lead of some sort. A simple cord looped under the collar with both ends in your hand is fine. Just turn one end loose as the puppy acknowledges the track. And, there are other fancier systems around from wire cables (not recommended) to a true Jager Slip Lead (Akah Leash) which while expensive and require a little learning curve and very useful. The Rule Book states that you can take your dog down the track for up to 30 meters but, unless you are tracking jack rabbits out west, the visual part of the track may not be much longer. The judges cannot evaluate the pup until you turn it loose so get the pup tied into the scent and release it after a few feet if testing on cottontail in the East.

I stress, again, the importance of this subject in your score. Optimally, you will spend a lot of time riding around looking for rabbits prior to the VJP and practice smoothly releasing the dog on the track.

Chapter Nine: The HZP

The test is for "young started dogs". It is not a test for the finished hunting dog and it is still considered a natural ability test. The natural ability test is really an evaluation of the mating that took place as opposed to an assessment of your individual dog. Of course, you are mostly interested in your dog and its score but, actually, as a breed club, we are evaluating the breeding behind the dog. See, if all the littermates are tested and their scores compared, breeders can determine if this was a good cross or not and this can lead to future breeding decisions. That is what these tests are all about. The problem is that the dog's training is a factor in its performance. Famous Drahthaar fancier, Jack Mansfield, told me once that he could take a mediocre dog and score high with it while I, as a rank amateur, could take a great dog and score poorly. So, yes, preparation is important. Let's look at a typical day at an HZP.

Like the VJP, the handlers and judges will gather for introductions, basic instructions, and encouragement early in the day. Then, the test will begin. Similar to the VJP, the judges will typically start with the Search subject, Gunfire Evaluation, and probably, Pointing. At this test, VR's are looking for a solid search effort and a more staunch pointing display. For a good score, you should be able to walk up to the dog and snap your leash on it as it remains pointing the game (but this is not required in the Rule Book...it just looks good.) Even at the HZP, the puppy can chase the flushed bird off without penalty. Remember, these are young, started dogs.

The judges will be evaluating Nose, i.e. the Use of Nose during the Search and Pointing subjects. Dogs that point over 10 meters from the game will show good use of nose. Dogs that crowd the bird will not score as well in the Nose evaluation so it is important as you train for the HZP to use the Halt or Whoa command when the dog first detects the scent cone.

Eventually, you will move to the Drag Field where a dead rabbit and a dead duck will be dragged by one of the VR's across a field. Your dog is required to track the dragged game and retrieve it to hand. The key to success here is a totally FF'd dog and practice on drags. There is an old cliché that dogs get bored with too many drags. In my experience, this hasn't happened primarily because I don't do enough of them I guess. But, a drag every 14 days or so is fine as long as the dog is completing them. Ideally, you recruit an assistant to do the drags for you. See, while the dog is tracking the game scent, your pup is also tracking the dragger too. So, varying individuals helps prepare the pup for a stranger's scent at the test. The dragging VR will hide in cover after dropping the game and, while judges do try to really hide, sparse cover may allow the dog to see the person. So, during practice, occasionally instruct the dragger to be only partially hidden so the dog gets used to seeing someone at the end of the track.

At the test, as you wait for your turn, take your duck(s) and rabbit(s) and let the dog smell of them one more time and even hold them in its mouth for a few seconds. Always show up with your own drag game; animals the dog is familiar with and has retrieved several times but don't bring nasty, worn out game animals. Rub your hands all over the game to put your scent on it too so the dog recognizes its old buddy duck or rabbit.

2 ducks or one? The rules allow you to provide two game animals for the drag; one to be dropped at the end and one to be placed near the dragger's feet. If the dog is in fact tracking the judge, it has a tendency to bypass the dropped animal and continue tracking to the dragger. If this happens, a duck/rabbit at the feet of the judge can allow a better chance of success. I recommend training with and providing two game animals for your drags. Of course, if you are training alone and the pup brings back the animal, there's one left out there. Good trainers recommend sending the pup again for the second one but usually, I just put the dog up and walk out there to get the remaining animal. There is more on this Drag subject in the VGP section.

Finally, you will move to the dreaded Water. To avoid duplication, I have included the Water subjects in detail in the following VGP section. So, prior to the HZP, flip down to the Water section of the VGP piece later in the book.

Chapter Ten: The VGP

General Comments

The Utility Test is one of endurance; not just at the test but in preparation for it. Oh, the dog doesn't mind it but, you, the trainer can get mentally and physically burned out as the weeks and months creep by. The key is to pace yourself. Get a written plan; a schedule and do your best to abide by it. The blood track is the show stopper at this test so perfect that early on. Water work is next in priority followed closely by Steadiness to Wing and Shot. While these are the big three in my experience, never forget that there are eight subjects under Obedience. So, when you are short on time or lazy, remember, there's always time for Obedience practice.

Memorize the VGPO. There are lots of subtleties in the Rule Book. For example, when placing your dog down for the Down Stay, the rules say "quietly"...silence is golden here. A simple hand signal for Down is optimal. There are dozens of these details in the VGPO, so be familiar with them.

Begin early accumulating the tools for VGP training. This includes a source of game: live ducks for Searches and birds for pointing work. In addition, you will need dead game particularly foxes or raccoons and rabbits. And, that old freezer for storing the dead animals. How are you going to transport live game to your training area? Look now for places to train. You will need large bodies of water with cover; a good Forest area, and some fields. What are you going to do for a Fox Box? Build one? Or, is one available to you nearby? Do you have a source of deer blood? You will need more than you think. And, you will need bottles for laying blood tracks. These are the questions that should be answered well before actual training starts.

One last suggestion before we get into the individual Subjects. About 30 days before the test dates, make a comprehensive list of items you will need to take with you to the test. I have included one in the Appendix for a guideline but this list is pretty much an individual creation. Each of us has their own needs and ideas. Just don't wait until the last minute to throw stuff in the truck and head out. You are going to be harried enough without forgetting your blood tracking leash.

[While these recommendations and rule listings are current as of the publication of this book, JGHV rules change almost annually as do the recommended interpretation of the regulations. Be sure and recheck the latest Rule Book(s) and current understanding of those rules.]

A review of the Regulations for Association Utility Test, the VGPO, commonly referred to as the "Rule Book" shows that the VGP is divided into four Subject Categories: Forest Work, Water Work, Field Work, and Obedience. Each of these Categories has a number of Subjects to which a multiplier is assigned. As a result, some Subjects can affect a dog's score more than others. In addition, some Subjects have required minimum scores that are required for each Prize category. The VGPO has a page dedicated to the formulas for each Prize. That is why you see some dogs with similar total scores but different Prize awards.

Forest Work

Blood Tracking[1]

The task of tracking a faint blood trail through the forest for 400 meters is the nemesis for many VGP candidates. But, it should not be because training for blood tracking is easy and fun.

Early tracking, on leash, should begin at age 12 weeks! Of course, these tracks are very short and simple. A can of Vienna sausages is opened and a short (10-15 feet) of the can's juices are used to lay the track. Small bits of the Vienna's are spaced a few inches apart along the short track. The puppy has a light cord-like leash on and you simply tell it to "track" or whatever command you like. Sure, it will struggle but it will learn that it needs to keep its head down to find the tasty treat and there is a scent line between them. One can purchase larger cans of Vienna's with little "bits" already prepared. They are nice to have.

Over weeks of course, you begin to lay longer and longer tracks with fewer and fewer treats. As the dog reaches adulthood, you will be amazed at how far it can follow these tracks.

Marty Ryan from Osseo Michigan and Mike Fortner from Forest City Arkansas have been excellent mentors for trainers around blood tracking. Much of the following information is gleaned from conversations and interactions with them.

It is not necessary to introduce blood early. Other items from just your own foot tracks to buttermilk to the Vienna sausage juice will teach the dog to follow a track and, more importantly, allow you to learn your dog's demeanor on a track and determine when the dog is on or off the track.

Contrary to many, accurate blood tracking is a forced, trained skill as opposed to merely a motivational one. Of course, there is a motivational component but, in the end, the dog performs better if he is taught the skill as a requirement. If you research information around training tracking dogs you will find that a huge component is the reward at the end of the track. While this is, in fact, a "motivational" tactic, over many tracks and many weeks of training, the "trained" tracker will become obvious.

All tracks should be marked so the trainer knows exactly where the scent line is located. This can be as simple as a field of short grass that leaves your footprints in an obvious manner or, more commonly, through the use of orange painted or white plastic clothespins in a wooded area. The field method is optimal because you know to the inch where the scent line is. In a forest area, the clothespin or other marker hangs on a nearby twig but the exact location of the scent deposit may be a foot or two away. We are looking for dogs that put their nose deep into the scent which requires that the trainer, in fact, knows where the scent is. Muddy fields are great for this situation.

In early training, food drops/treats are useful. The treats should be spaced fairly closed together early on but hidden to a degree on the track. The term used is "kicked in" which just means the treats are under cover of dirt, leaves, or other debris to force the dog to look close to find it. This teaches the dog to put its nose deep into the scent deposit. In the Deep South, these hidden treats are quickly overcome by insects, especially ants. This can be prevented by a visit to your local veterinarian and ask them for six 13 dram pills vials. If you are a regular client, they will probably be free. Put the treat in the vial, close it tightly and hide it along the track. When the dog finds it, open it and give them the treat.

While the overall approach is one of obedience and trained tracking, praise for the dog is crucial when performing correctly. A key word or phrase like "good boy" or "good girl" should be instituted early in life. For example, every time you use the phrase a reward treat is given. Over time, the dog will associate the phrase with pleasure and understand its meaning. Then, when the dog finds the treats hidden along the track, lots of good boys or good girls reinforce optimal performance. If the dog gets off the track, a correction word like "Ahnnt" should be used but not in a punishing manner. We want our dogs to enjoy blood tracking and not dread it. Marty Ryan suggests 10 praise words for each one correction.

Initial training should just be tracking you; your scent. Starting in a mown or plowed field or even your lawn, the dog will soon learn to follow your tracks all over the place. Gradually, you move to strange areas and longer and longer foot tracks. You will be amazed. Early on, make your foot tracks deep and scuff your feet to allow lots of scent to be left behind. Use lots of treats too and work in a straight line for a while, say 30-40 yards. As your training progresses, provide a more likely scenario with fewer and fewer treats spaced farther and farther apart and more and more turns in the track. Do not go too fast in your training. First, the track gets longer. Then, there are fewer treats. Then, comes the turns. Try not to get all the distractions included in the first more difficult tracks.

If the dog gets off the track, don't push the dog forward but back up to the last area that the dog was sure of the track and begin again. Slow and steady is the mantra.

Many dogs, especially the great field searchers, want to work with their head up. Excellent blood trackers have their head down and their nose deep into the scent line. Learning to read your dog's posture and head/nose position is crucial because at the test, you won't have a clue where the track is and you will be totally dependent on reading your dog to confirm that you are on the correct track. Good blood trackers work with their bodies in line with the track as opposed to at a right angle to the track. They are astraddle of it. Dogs that are swinging back and forth on the tracking lead with their head up are usually off the track. However, in my experience, it is difficult to have a great searching hunting dog and a great blood tracker in one package. Early on, you will note your dog's strengths and weaknesses. That perfect dog is rare. But, hard, wide searching dogs can learn to blood track and pass the VGP requirement. One just has to learn the dog's style, tracking system, and be able to determine when the dog is off the track by those parameters.

Obviously, to train your dog to track blood, you have to lay the training track correctly. Good trainers lay a "bed" or "scent pad" at the beginning with lots of foot scuffing and depositing as much scent as possible off your feet to get the dog's nose's attention. In the earliest training efforts, walking the track two or three times is often advisable. You simply walk the track out to the goal, scuffing your feet in every step then turn and scuff your feet as you walk back to the beginning. While blood or other scent source is not needed at this point in my experience, including blood earlier than later is a good thing. I have changed my tactics around this and now start putting blood out after the puppy has learned to track on lead. Typically, in early training, a food treat every 3-5 feet is recommended. If possible, lay the track into the wind so the dog can smell the treats up ahead. In this earliest training, it is fine for the dog to watch you lay the track. At this point, you are just trying to let the dog know what the game is and what is expected. I like to actually scuff the food treat into the ground like the basic foot tracks.

At the end of the track, there should be a special reward, i.e. food. Many items are used from fast-food hamburgers to pieces of venison to my favorite, a can of Vienna sausage (unopened). The canned product keeps ants and other vermin from contaminating the reward as you track to it. I also like a few wieners in a zip-loc bag. These can be used as hidden treats along the track. German trainers train for blood tracking on an empty stomach ostensibly to encourage the dog to find the food at the end of the track. I have not found that to be required but might be useful for some dogs. In the forest, be sure and mark the track with flagging, clothespins or other items to insure that you know where the track is at all times. Otherwise, you will be struggling with the timing of corrections. Learn to grab these markers as your dog follows the track. This makes landowners happier but also avoids confusion if you lay another track there days later and find random abandoned markers in the area.

Every track should begin with a ritual. Typically, handlers put their dog down about 3 feet from the beginning of the track. This allows the dog to inhale the maximum scent as it lies in wait. William Koehler, one of the early writers about tracking dogs, recommended the dog be left in this down position for two full minutes so he can check and recheck all the scents around him. Remove the standard collar (required at the test) and place the tracking collar and tracking lead on the dog at this time to signal "we're doing another blood track!"

Although you can use the regulation 30 foot long blood tracking leash, you should, at this point, have a grip up close and personal, say 3 feet back from the dog. Often, a shorter leash is handier at this stage of training.

Using your command of "Track" or "Blood", begin the track while stepping forward toward the first treat. At this point, real tracking is not the issue. You are just trying to teach the dog what you want it to do and to obey you. But, walk slowly. Pour on the praise words at this point. This teaches the dog that "Hey, I am doing what my owner wants me to do". If the dog gets off the track, say one body length, use your correction word "No" or "Ahhnt" followed by your tracking command and lots of praise as the dog relocates the scent line. Tone of voice is important. Soft, steady praise commands encourages soft, steady work.

Prong collars may be of value for dogs that pull too aggressively or even just a sharp jerk on the standard tracking collar. In my experience, they just confuse the dog and may make them want to "Heel". Try not to drag the dog back to the scent. Let him/her find it and then heap on the praise.

After the dog has located the end of the track and eaten its food reward, heap lots of praise and petting on it. This signals a positive end to the session and encourages the dog for future training.

It is fine to lay several tracks per training session. As the dog progresses, you can space the treats more apart and make the tracks longer and longer. Repeat these easy tracks as much as possible, hopefully 2-4 tracks per day for 14 straight days. Your goal is to complete a 200 yard straight track into the wind with treats only every 40 feet by day 14. Never allowing pulling (difficult with those hard searching dogs) and never allow a dog to skip a treat. They must find each and every tidbit. Even for dogs fairly advanced in their blood tracking, treat tracks, even in the lawn, encourages a slower pace and can be useful even up to the test dates.

After the 200 yard track is completed successfully, the next distraction is wind. Begin laying tracks with a crosswind first followed by tracks with the wind to your back. The next distraction is turns or corners. Initially, just one turn but at a sharp 90° angle is sufficient. Marty Ryan recommends triple laying around the corner, i.e. scuff your feet over the track three times to help the dog make the turn. Eventually, of course, you should be able to stop that tactic. Once your dog is proficient at making a right turn, change to a left turn for a few tracks. Some trainers think most dogs are "right-handed" and tend to look to the right first. I have not documented that in my own dogs but starting with a right turn doesn't hurt anything.

Finally, you should lay a "box track". As you might surmise, this track is 100 yards to a corner, another 100 yards to a corner, and a final corner back to the beginning. This allows three good turns plus a varying wind direction. Many trainers are not using blood at this point but, for me, I am including it; blood plus treats is optimal for me. If you have the time, you should be able to complete this training regime in six weeks.

It is also nice to provide the dog with more dramatic distractions like a dead duck or rabbit lying a few feet off the track. When the dog turns to go to the animal, correct it and get it back on the track. There will never be a track for the dog that does not have a distraction. A flock of turkeys, deer, rabbits and box turtles can all cross the blood track at the test. It is imperative that the dog be trained to ignore distractions.

Eventually, if you haven't already done so, you want to introduce blood. Deer blood is ideal but hog or cow blood will work. You should begin collecting blood months in advance. It freezes well. Package it in small bottles for easy thawing and training use. I often dilute the blood 50:50 with water to use less of the precious blood and, if a dog can track diluted blood, it can surely track the full-strength stuff. For the finest tracking dog, late in training, gaps of 15 or 20 feet between blood drops are in order. Mark the track well and when the dog reaches the gap and struggles, help him/her through the gap. This teaches the dog that there may be gaps when tracking a shot game animal and it must persevere to find the scent.

On the day of the test, regardless of your training preparation, this subject can be intimidating. The judges will lay the track early in the morning and at least 2 hours later, you and your dog will be asked to follow the track(**§20-24**). There will be a "wound bed" at the beginning and a small paper sign nearby documenting the time the track was laid. Usually, there is a number on this card too and you will have drawn for the numbered track assignment. While there may be some blood along the track that you can see, often, especially in sandy soils, you will see very little blood. If you, in fact, do see blood, you can either drop a marker (cotton ball) or verbally advise the judge that you just saw blood and they will mark it for you. This can be important because if you get totally lost, you can always ask to go back to the location that you last saw blood. This will not count as a restart if you do it on your own without the judges advising you that you have veered over 60 m off the track.

The equipment you use for blood tracking is also important. A "regulation" blood tracking collar is about 1 ½ to 2 inches wide and often have a special swivel on them for leash attachment. Really, any wide collar that the dog can identify as its "blood tracking collar" is fine but a true tracking collar is a nice purchase. Experts do not slip the collar over the dog's head to begin tracking although it is a very convenient thing to do. The collar should fit a little more snugly than that to prevent it slipping off the dog's head during the task or chasing after a wounded animal if it approaches it while tracking. Other collars must be removed prior to beginning the track. Have a pocket available for that collar or ask one of the judges to keep it for you. The blood tracking leash is more important. Most traditionalist use a flat leather leash at least 6 meters (19 feet) long but longer is preferable because the VGPO requires that the handler's hands be at least 19 feet from the dog. It is unhandy to do blood tracking at the very end of the leash, so some excess is optimal. Do not make the judges continually correct you for being too close to the dog. A knot or marker of some type on the leash at the 19 foot spot will help you stay behind that on the leash. Leather leashes do require good care and maintenance. A rather stiff rope-type leash is also good because this leash is much less likely to get tangled in underbrush; is comfortable on the hand, and very durable. Leashes. I have had poor luck with Permatack leashes; notorious for getting tangled in saplings.

The track will go straight for about 100 m before the first turn. The angle of the turn will be obtuse, i.e. greater than 90° and there will another one as well as some type of wound bed along the track. This wound bed is often not visibly evident but there will be excess blood there. Only ¼ liter of blood will be used over the 400 m track! This is about 8.5 ounces, a little over ½ pint. Again, you probably won't see much blood but your dog will smell it. This means the dog often knows more about where the track is than you do. Of course, some logic is in order. If you just came from one direction and you are at a loss, you know that the track does not go back that way. They can't lay an acute angle in the track so it is probably not to the sharp right or left, so it must be somewhere in an arc in front of you. Go back to the last place you found blood, and think a minute. There is no time limit on blood tracking in the VGPO but, of course, you must eventually move on. There are usually other dogs to test. Again, if you are totally lost, and your dog is prepared, trust the dog.

At the end of the track, a dead big-game animal will be found. The judges will ask you to place your dog in the down position and everyone will walk off for a few minutes to see if the dog will maul the game. There is nothing in the VGPO that states how you must place the dog, so put its rear end toward the game. The type of game varies from test to test and can be anything the Test Director had available as long as it has cloven hooves. Typically, it will be a deer but I have seen pigs or goats used. Just be aware of this and insure that your dog will show little interest in the animal and certainly will not maul it. A solid, positive Down command, albeit quietly, is the key to success at this point.

All blood tracks that are called "day tracks" (by far the most common testing method) will be between 2 and 5 hours old. While five hours might seem old to you, your dog will probably do an overnight track just as easily. In fact, training on overnight tracks can be a good strategy. Tracks may be laid by either the drip method or the dab method. I have not been able to see any difference in dog performance between the two methods. If you must train for every contingency, use both methods in training but, again, if your dog is a trained blood-tracker, he/she will follow either method.

Judges are well-versed in blood tracking. Some handlers may tell you that one judge will always be standing on the track and another one will follow you if you get off the track. Nowadays, this rarely happens. Typically, all the judges will follow you as you wander willy-nilly off the track. But, they will know where the track is! Almost all judges have a map in their pocket describing the track..."just to left of red rock...over downed hickory tree.....around edge of large puddle...etc. or a GPS device handy with the track recorded. Regardless, it is futile to try and ascertain the location of the track based on where the judges are standing. They have all been there and done all this before and know all the tricks.

If you get off the track more than 60 meters, the judges will advise you and get you back to the track. You get two of these "restarts" but your score will go down 1 predicate, i.e. from Very Good to Good and so on, with each call back. The third time you and your dog get off 60 meters, you are done and fail the subject and the test. Again, keep calm! Trust your dog! And use logic: where did the track start; there are two turns, so the end should be in "that" direction somewhere. Realistically, the judges had to put that dead animal out there and they will have to move it for the next dog. Logic says the animal is probably near a road, path, or trail of some kind. Help your dog find it. Exude confidence as you and your dog follow the track. While it is perfectly fine to stop the dog and offer water or just a short rest, continual "downing" and looking for blood yourself might decrease your score. Even if you are scared to death, act like you know what you are doing. In many instances, you actually do and the dog is on the track. Some dogs love blood tracking and can get pretty excited on the track. This may make them less obedient if you do "Down" them. If they refuse, don't continue to give the Down command. This will lower your Obedience score. Just give them a Sit and, hopefully, they will acquiesce.

If the leash accidently slips out of your hand, call you dog immediately!! Otherwise, they are off and running down the blood track. To prevent this, keep a firm grip on the leash and hang on! Yes, this does happen! Don't panic (like I did) but hit that whistle, get the dog back and act like everything is routine. Get the dog back on the track and go forward.

Keep in mind, judges will go through whatever underbrush and terrain that is necessary to complete a regulation blood track. Wear a tight fitting cap. They are easily brushed off during the track and it breaks the dog's concentration if you have to stop and pick it up. Make sure your boot laces are tight. You don't want to stop and tie your shoes midway through the track. If you do, in fact, see blood, the simplest thing to do is say "Marking Blood" and the judges will mark it for you. But, you cannot mumble it! Say it loud enough for the judges to hear it as you follow your dog.

Training for blood tracking is fun and fairly easy. You can do it by yourself without an assistant. You can do it around the house if you have any room at all. Of course, you will eventually be putting out blood; waiting 2-5 hours; and trying the track but it can be done at a leisurely pace albeit with regularity. Don't forget that reward at the end of every practice track. Since this Subject is crucial for passing the VGP, I may overdo it but I try to put my dog on a blood track at least weekly over the summer prior to the test. My goal is usually a minimum of 20 tracks in practice. However, as the test nears, your dog may get faster and faster on the tracks because they've got the game down to a, well, a game. I do stop doing them about two weeks prior to the test unless the dog is still struggling.

A short mention of two options for blood trackers needs to be included. Dead Game Baying (*Totverbellen*) and Dead Game Guiding (*Totverweisen*) are available for testing at the VGP. In these tasks, the dog is released without a leash and asked to find the game animal on its own after it has completed the standard on lead track. The handlers and two judges will remain at the second wound bed. No voice, whistle, or other signals may be used to help the dog. The dog has ten minutes to find the dead animal and report either via barking or by bringing a device called a *brinsingel* to the handler in its mouth. While few people attempt these extra steps, the *totverweisen* (bringing back the brinsingel) is a straightforward training extension of the Forced Fetch and is doable. Dogs that are bayers need to develop this trait early in puppyhood by barking for food and treats. For an in-depth look at totverbellen, see the Summer, 2010 issue of the VDD-GNA Newsletter where Bryon Beaton provided an excellent treatise on training this valuable skill. If you have interest in totverbellen, it is strongly suggested that you reference Bryon's article.

One last point: For a "very good" score, a calm, thorough working dog is essential. Excessive and unrestrained speed can lower the score. So, from day one, try to keep the dog from going too fast down the track with either a pinch collar or at least calm voice commands to encourage steady work.

Fox Over Obstacle

In the US, either a fox or a raccoon can be used in this subject. While retrieving the fox is neat and more traditional, the raccoon is more readily available and most dogs prefer it to the odiferous fox. Either a "box" or a ditch may be used at the test. The box must be at least 70 cm high and the ditch must be at least 80 cm deep. The ditch must be at least 1 meter across too. The handler must stand at least 5 meters from the obstacle when releasing the dog. The dog must jump the obstacle, retrieve the animal, and return to the handler with the animal on one command. Again, this entire subject is an extension of the

Forced Fetch command. While relatively easy to do, it is important because the dog must score at least a "sufficient" in either this task or the Fox Drag to pass the test. The "fox in the box" is less risky, so handlers should have this perfected in training to insure eventual passing of the VGP test.

Training for this subject is straightforward but, obviously, you need an obstacle. Serious trainers will build a box. The dimensions are in the VGPO. Boxes are also available at most training days organized by the various chapters but your own box is very handy.

At the test, for goodness sake, bring your own animal. The fox or raccoon should be one that your dog is familiar with and has retrieved many times. Foxes must weigh at least 7.7 pounds or 3.5kg and have their tail still attached to be legal in this test. Don't just toss the animal in the box but step over in the box and place the animal in a dramatic manner while your dog watches from its sitting position 5-6 m away. Place the animal to make the retrieve as easy as possible for your dog, i.e. tail to right and head to left parallel to the front of the box about 12 inches from the front. This gives the dog room to turn around and pick up the fox or raccoon with ease and encourages it to face you after lifting the animal. Your dog will be scored on its manner of retrieve on this subject too, so train for a nice sit, look you in the eye, and give up the animal freely, again, an extension of the Forced Fetch.

Drags

Through the HZP and the VGP, we still see dogs that struggle with the Furred Game Drag and even the Feathered Game Drag. At the VGP in the Forest Category, your dog will be asked to track and retrieve a dead raccoon or fox and a dead rabbit for 300 m through the woods, pick it up and bring it back to you.

Practicing for drags is fun and easy to do. You don't have to have live game and just need a place to do the exercise. But, that can backfire because dogs can get bored with drags over time. As a result, don't just do drag after drag. Space these practice sessions out to avoid complacency on the dog's part. Initial short drags for a puppy should be straight and about 50 m long. Begin early on telling the puppy "It is a drag". They will learn this phrase and know what is going on as they approach the start. Gradually increasing the distance and adding turns will produce a competent fur or feather drag retriever. This subject mimics a wounded bird or rabbit that scooted off after the shot. Good versatile dog owners and, really, all hunters should not leave edible game in the field. Eventually, you want to do a drag that is a true "box", i.e. it starts and goes 75 m, makes a right angle, another leg of about 75 m, and ends near the start or even goes behind the start. If a dog can complete that type of puzzle, it will do well in the testing format. Additionally, after a puppy has learned the basics of the drag subject, keep your drags to about the regulation distance, i.e. about 300 m for fur and 200 m for feathered drags. I don't think the dog actually counts its steps or can measure the distance but after many, many drags, it will know that the object is supposed to be "about here".

Some dogs, after the long "drag" in the Forest, have difficulty coming back to the handler. They get disoriented. I don't know any way to solve this except do more drags. It can be scary when your dog returns with the game 75 yards away and looks the other way. You cannot give a correction command, only a light "good dog" if the dog is coming toward you. Just don't have a heart attack if this happens and give your dog a chance to find you.

Again, you should show up with your own game, clean and presentable for the judges and your dog. While it is acceptable to use just one game animal, most trainers prefer to have two of each. The rationale is simple: while the dog is tracking the scent of the dead animal, it is also tracking the judge's scent too. The animal at the judge's feet is the dragged game and the carried game is placed at the end of the drag unless the handler requests differently. There is no known disadvantage to using two animals except that you have to have two animals instead of one. Plus, there is one subtle judgment call around this situation too. If there is just one animal at the end of the drag and the dog bypasses it or even refuses to pick it up either through carelessness, poor nose, or other issues, the judge can disqualify the dog because "it left edible game" even if it was going to eventually find it (who knows). But, if there is another animal at his or her feet, there is a question as to the dog smelling the second animal as opposed to leaving the dragged game. If, on the other hand, there is only one fox, raccoon, or rabbit, and the dog bypasses it initially, the judge may elect to fail the animal. In reality, most judges will give the dog some time to locate the animal and pick it up. This is a minor point, but trivia makes perfection and perfection is no trivia. The problem with using two animals is that you need to train with two animals. To introduce two animals on the day of the test could be risky and an incident where the dog tried to pick up both animals or spit one out and went back and forth between the pair has been reported. So, if we are going to test with two animals, we need to train with two animals. This brings on more talk because there will be two animals out there and you will have to go all the way to the end of the 300 m drag to fetch the remaining one yourself after training. This can be a burden because, if you are like most folks, you are trying to get as much training as possible in a day and that is a time consumer. The optimal approach is to hire someone to do your drags for you and let them take two animals every time. Then, they can bring the un-retrieved one back. But, the alternative is to resend the dog for the second animal! After completion of the first retrieve of the drag, simply sit the dog down and send it again. Thereby, getting two practice drags for the price of one. While this approach is used by some excellent trainers, it could lead to confusion on the dog's part: "Am I supposed to bring them both back?" As a result, I train with two animals but either my buddy brings the second one back or, heck, I just walk out there and get the thing. At the test, you can choose which animal you want dragged and which one you want left near the judge but you need to advise the dragging judge before he starts the track.

Again, the animals you provide for the judges should be clean and as fresh as possible. Don't show up with decomposing game for a judge to drag.

Many handlers approach the start of the track and just loose their dog. A better tactic is to walk the dog down the track on lead prior to release. The VGPO states that the dog can work the track for 20 m on lead so use as much of this leeway as possible. A handler can restart his dog three times without finding the game but each restart lowers the score one predicate. Even a simple encouragement like "track 'em" can be considered a restart by critical judges. After the dog has found the game and is returning with it, no corrections or admonitions are allowed. Some gentle "good boy's" or "good girl's" are usually allowed but even these should be done with decorum. As a judge, I dislike a handler who loudly yells "Good Boy" from the time he sees the dog returning. Waving your hands and yelling to the dog just shows less than optimal preparation. This appears to be more of a harsh semi-correction than a calming encouragement. A harsh or even quiet "Here" can get you in real trouble. To show the optimal preparation, nothing should be said at all.

If your dog seems reluctant to sit and give up the game, just take it from him and put him on lead. Do not give multiple "Sit" commands and do not allow the dog to parade around with the game. If this happens, and the dog is within a few feet of you, just step over to the dog and get the game. Your Manner of Retrieve score will be lowered for that incident but that is better than the dog dropping the game or, heaven forbid, taking it off to the gallery. In my experience, dogs that are sloppy in their first few retrieves generally continue the trend over the test and often their Manner of Retrieve deteriorates as the test goes on.

Dogs that bury or eat game will be disqualified from the test. To prevent this, a solid without-a-doubt approach to Force Fetching must have been employed during that phase of training. The dog must know that it is to find the game, bring it back with a correct hold on the animal, sit and deliver it freely every time. Complete, total Force Fetching will prevent dogs from doing anything else with the game. Dogs that have been too severely trained and disciplined at the final retrieve stages may develop a reluctance to approach the handler with the game and bury it rather than get another session of reprimand. The line between a good trainer and a bad one is thin. Don't fall into the trap of making the delivery of game dreadful for the dog while you insist on perfect performance in daily training. At the test, as soon as you take the animal from the dog, give to a judge and get the leash on your dog. Then, take the animal from the judge and return to your truck but do not let your dog run around after the task, jumping up for the animal, etc. This could hurt your obedience score. If the dog insists on jumping for the animal, give it a Sit command then Heel it off to your vehicle.

Independent Search (*Stöbern*)(§§48-55)

For this subject, the dog will be asked to search thoroughly and methodically a wooded thicket or area of forest. The rationale behind this task is that the area could be surrounded by hunters and the dog is asked to route the game out for a shot by one of the standers or a dead animal could be located in the thicket.

To train for this subject, begin by placing an object, e.g. a training dummy about 30 m out in a wooded area. Bring your dog to the wood line and command "Search". The dog should find the dummy fairly quickly and return with it. Over a period of days, you extend the location of the dummy until it is about 100 m out in the area. Eventually, placing as many as three dummies scattered in the area will improve the dog's searching performance. When they bring one back, send them out again and again until they find all three dummies. This teaches them to search the entire area which is required for a high score.

At the test, one judge will stay with you while two will place themselves at or near the corners of the area to be searched. For the highest score, all three judges must see your dog on multiple occasions diligently searching for game. Once the dog learns that there are three dummies out there during training, you can send them back each time they bring one in (for the first two). Eventually, the dog will understand the game and look and look to find the dummies. At the test, of course, there will not be any dummies but the dog will not know that and will search the entire area to find the object that has always been there before. Typically, judges mentally divide the area into quadrants and they want to see the dog in all four quadrants multiple times for the highest score. The judge that is standing with you will also evaluate the dog's persistence and meticulous work.

An additional training tactic that can solidify a good score is the use of "fake judges" during training. Recruit two buddies and give them each a dead duck or rabbit. They then place themselves 100 m in a forest area on opposite corners. When the dog comes by them, they toss the game animal in front of the dog. The dog will pick it up and, surely, return it to you, the handler. Resend the dog until it finds the second person who repeats the game toss. After a few repetitions, the dog understands that "I gotta find that guy out there with that duck". Then, at the test, the dog again looks for your buddies (this time they are real judges) allowing both VR's to see the dog which is the key to getting a "4" in this subject.

One risk during the stöbern is chasing game, especially deer, out of the area and not returning within a reasonable time, especially if it fails to respond to whistle or voice commands. The judges are looking for finished hunting dogs that are obedient and exceptions can be excluded from the test. Generally, the judges moving to their position will move game out before the dog is sent but there is always a chance. To avoid failure, your dog should be trained to return to you on a whistle even if it is chasing game.

To insure this, place an electronic collar on your dog and ride around late in the afternoon looking for deer feeding or moving. When a deer is seen, let your dog approach the area, find the scent and take off on it. Once the dog is "running" the deer, give two or three strong blasts on your whistle and give collar stimulation as a moderately high level. Continue this pressure until the dog returns to your side. A few trips like this will instill the recall to the whistle command even when on game.

Dense Cover Search (*Buschieren*)(§§56-58)

The Dense Cover Search is one of the most neglected training subjects for the VGP. The so-called "dense" cover varies with the test site and may or may not be really "dense". Regardless, the dog should know what the phrase "hunt close" means. This can be taught during normal hunting, especially when you are looking for downed game. If the dog hears that command regularly, it will learn that you want it to stay in close. In the Dense Cover Search subject, the judges will evaluate the dog's handling nature as well as its calm, methodical searching style. Keep your commands minimal and quiet; be calm yourself. Optimally, no commands are given. The dog should work slow enough that you can see it most of the time and easily keep up with it. A dog that checks by its handler frequently is impressive but one that leaves the area in a wide search will not score as well. You, or the judges, will have to fire at least one shot (sometime two) over the dog during this subject. This is a good thing because most dogs will come quickly to the shot which helps keep them in close.

For the highest score, you should prepare your dog by actually doing some dense cover searches prior to the test. Use the phrase "Hunt Close" and if the dog gets out too far, correct it either with the electronic collar or a whistle command.

Minimum Requirements in the Forest

For a Prize 1, the dog must score a "very good" on its blood track and at least a sufficient in all the other subjects with a minimum score of 90 in the Forest. For a Prize 2, the blood tracking must be at least a "good" along with sufficient in the other subjects and a minimum of 80 total points. For a Prize 3, the dog must score at least a sufficient in all the subjects except the fox/raccoon drag or the Fox Over Obstacle subject. The minimum score for a Prize 3 is 48 points in the Forest work.

Water Work

A finished utility dog must be a dependable retriever of all edible game but especially waterfowl. The pond or lake that you will test in will be at least 6 meters wide (They are always wider than that) and deep enough to require the dog to swim. Your dog will be required to make three retrieves of ducks at the VGP.

Gunshot Soundness (§70)

The Gun Sensitivity or Gunshot Soundness Test will be conducted first. A shot (dead) duck is thrown out in the water in full view of the dog. The handler commands the dog to retrieve the duck and it must complete this retrieve. The dog has "about 1 minute" to enter the water after the lone command is given. While the dog is swimming to the duck, a live round will be fired into the water around the dead duck. You cannot give another command during this retrieve. If your dog fails to get the duck and bring it to you, it will fail the test and cannot continue.

The vast majority of dogs will certainly swim out and get a dead duck that they've seen hit the water. If a dog is hesitant about this task, it is questionable that it will make a finished retriever. While this task is very straightforward, it still pays to practice it several times prior to the test. The dog needs to know and become used to the loud report of the gun fired fairly close to it.

Blind Retrieve (§71)

The Blind Retrieve from Dense Cover is a straightforward task also. As retrieves go, it has to be considered simple. However, every year, dogs fail this portion of the test. Assuming your dog has passed the HZP, this retrieve will typically duplicate the HZP task with a somewhat longer retrieve being common. Also, assuming your dog is totally trained around the Forced Fetch, this requirement should be accomplished without issues.

The bottom line on this task (as well as all other water retrieves) is that the dog must know that the object, i.e. the duck is always on the far shore or, at the least, there is a duck out there. Beginning with very short retrieves, say just 10 meters, the duck is always placed in cover across the water even if it is only a very short distance. The typical failure involves a dog swimming out 10-20 meters and beginning to swim around in a circle. This is invariably caused by the handler throwing dummies for their dog in daily training. Every dog will get training dummy after dummy that is thrown for it. There is no rationale in continuing to do this even though it is fun to watch your dog swim out and bring a dummy back. After the initial introduction to water, we never throw a dummy for our dog that he can see hit. It is all about the blind retrieve.

In previous chapters, the drills for the blind retrieve were addressed in detail. These drills should be repeated during training using a dead duck as the object. Consistent repetition of these drills will insure success. At the test, the exact same format must be employed. Walk the dog up to the starting point, say Sit.... Dead Bird... and, when the dog looks in the correct direction say...Good and quickly say Back. The dog will swim straight across the water to the area of the duck, smell around and find the duck; bring it back to you and sit and deliver it freely to hand.

Dogs vary in their willingness or ability to "line" to an object. If your dog is not a good "liner" then lots of lining drills are in order before the VGP. Then, at the test, check the wind and try to send your dog just downwind of the duck. If it passes the duck upwind, there is a chance it will go deeper into the cover or even up on the shore which will cause you tons of anxiety.

If, for some reason, the dog misses the duck and begins an inordinate search maybe up on the shore or even swimming down the pond, you are allowed to help and direct your dog but constant influence lowers the score. You can throw a "stone" to cause a splash near the hidden game. Each time you throw an object, your score falls substantially. The question all handlers have to ask themselves is "When should I throw the stone?" There just is not hard and fast rule for this. You will know your dog and you must be able to read the situation. Typically, if the dog is still in the area and looking, we refrain from admitting defeat and do not throw the dreaded stone. But, if the dog has been working on the retrieve for quite some time...say 10 minutes, you can ask the judges "How much time do I have?" There is no set time limit on the Blind Retrieve but, obviously, there comes a time when it is not happening. In my estimate, stones are thrown for VGP Blind Retrieves in less than 10% of the cases, so be cautious. And, remember, if you are going to throw a stone, your penalty is no more for a big rock than a small pebble. If you are going to do it, make it count. As suggested in earlier chapters, it is recommended a handler go to the Blind Retrieve task with two golf balls in their pocket. Golf balls can be thrown more accurately, sink readily (you don't want him to bring the thrown object back!) and create a decent splash. As stated earlier, you should have thrown a very few of these "stones" in practice to let the dog know that a splash means go over there. But, for goodness sake, keep this to a minimum. I have seen some handlers wait and wait while their dog struggles in this subject, primarily at the HZP level. By the time they elect to throw the stone, they have already deteriorated to a lower predicate anyway. Just know your dog and know its capabilities. Yes, I have seen handlers throw the stone as the dog enters the water the first time.

What about just using hand signals? DD's are supposed to find the duck with their nose but, generally, judges won't penalize you for giving light hand signals. Verbal commands will hurt you and too many of them could cause a failure. But, if you have taught your dog to respond to directional hand signals, e.g. an arm pointing toward the duck, and things are not going well, this is worth a try. Again, don't make a big deal out of it and be subtle. Also, you can walk along the shore a few feet. Some judges are stricter than others about this but walking a few steps toward the area of the duck is often permissible. During practice sessions, get in the habit of staring at the area of the duck. Then, at the test, stare intently at the desired location. Over months of water retrieves, your dog may figure out that the handler is looking where the duck is!

The Search Without a Duck (§69)

To document the dog's propensity for diligent searching and its love of water work, Utility dogs are asked to search a pond on command even though there is no game present. The judges will examine the pond to insure that there are no native ducks, coots, or other water birds on the pond before beginning this subject.

The dog should enter the water without hesitation and independently search the cover on one command e.g. "Search". While the handler may help the dog with hand and voice signals in this subject, continually harking the dog into an area will lower your score. Again, keep it light and calm and don't overdo it. Frankly, most dogs don't need much help if they have been trained well. Judges will observe the dog for about ten minutes to certify their score. The key to this subject is lots of live duck searches so the dog thinks there must be a duck out here because there always has been one. The dog should cover the pond completely; searching all sides of the pond and cover in the middle of the water. As outlined in the next subject, the way to get a wide, impressive search is to practice in wide, impressive water. Judges and handlers can walk up to a pond and tell quickly if it is "4H" water or not. It is hard to get "4H"in "3" water.

Realistically, most trained dogs figure out pretty quickly that there "ain't nuthin" here. Judges vary in their evaluation of this subject but, unless the dog just doesn't go in the water at all, most judges will give a Good to Very Good evaluation.

Search Behind a Live Duck (§72)

In this subject, a live duck is tossed a few yards out into the water after its flight feathers have been removed. Your dog will not be allowed to see this but you can observe it from your vehicle. The judges will toss stones, shoot slingshots, and generally "shoo" the duck away until it has gone out of sight, generally to the far shore. You will bring your dog up the water's edge and give the command "Search" or similar. When I first studied this subject, I questioned whether a dog could actually track scent on the water. After observing many, many tests and training episodes, I now have no doubt that our dogs can, in fact, follow a duck's scent on water. This is the goal of this subject. Even if the dog loses the scent line, it will begin a, hopefully, long and diligent search of the pond and its banks to find the live duck. Once it is discovered, the duck will try to evade the dog as it chases it and usually barks like crazy. One of the judges will shoot the duck and the dog must retrieve it.

Keep in mind, the Subject is "searching behind a live duck" so many judges look for the dog actually tracking the duck's escape route. This is what is needed for the best score. Many will tell you that it is better if the dog just does a big search and doesn't find the duck but, in my experience, that has not been true.

If the dog is determined to have seen the duck, it is considered to have found it and must retrieve it either in shot form or, if it catches it, in the live state. If the judges conclude, after several minutes of impressive searching but without actually finding the duck, that they have seen enough, they can end the search and award a score. [Note: at the HZP, each dog must have three retrieves in the water. If the dog fails to actually find the duck, a dead duck will be tossed in the water as the dog returns to its handler and the dog must retrieve that duck. At the VGP, this is not required.]

There is no secret for training for this subject. One just needs to provide plenty of live duck searches over the summer as one trains for the VGP. However, there is no need for a live duck every time you train at the water. One or two ducks per month should be more than sufficient for the vast majority of dogs. To provide optimal training, find the largest ponds available with cover. The larger the water, the wider the dog will typically search. To train in a small farm pond on a regular basis will probably restrict the dog's tendency to perform a wide, exciting search. As the test date nears, it might be wise to decrease the exposure to live ducks to help insure the dog does not get too used to the subject but rather anticipates a good duck search and chase with a lot of excitement and drive.

Water Work Scoring: For a Prize I, a dog must have passed the gun sensitivity test and have at least a "Sufficient" performance in all the other water tasks; leading to a minimum score of 36 points in the water. For a Prize II, they must have at least 30 total water work points and for a Prize III, the minimum is 22 points. Again, all dogs must pass the gun sensitivity to pass the test. If the dog fails on a duck retrieve, the dog cannot continue to be tested. Keep in mind, the Search Behind a Live Duck is an exercise in tracking. To search and not find the duck is of minimal value but, if the dog shows a long, diligent search, it can still get a good score. The Independent Search Without a Duck subject demonstrates the dog's *searching* ability so optimally, the dog will, in fact, find the duck during the Live Duck task.

Field Work

There are six subjects under field work: Nose, Search, Pointing, Manners Behind Game, Blind Retrieve of Feathered Game, and a score on their Manner of Retrieve on that feathered game.

Nose (§§ 76-77)

While there is little a trainer can do to improve a dog's use of Nose, certainly, hunting and exposure to the environment wakes up the dog's brain and scenting ability. Dogs recognize scent by dissolving scent droplets or vapor in their nose where it contacts nerve sensors which send a signal to the dog's brain that says "Hey, that's a quail!" In order for this to happen, the nose must be very moist because water is needed to dissolve the scent vapor molecules. Thus, it makes sense to keep your dog well hydrated before and during the test. A simple water bottle is a start but insuring water consumption the night before the test is more important. Exposing the dog to many and varied terrains and types of cover also expands the dog's use of nose along with repeated exposure to game.

Search (§78)

Search is all about the "will to find", game that is. To find game, a dog must search diligently but the actual range the dog utilizes is not as important as a systematic approach to a given cover. If a dog is cast in an open field, the judges will appreciate a wide, "big" search but if released in a thicket, an adaptable dog will come in close and check likely game spots as it searches.

Unlike the natural ability tests, dogs will also be evaluated on their willingness to be handled and their obedience to commands as they search. During the VGP test, dogs are evaluated for obedience from the time they appear at the test until the test is over. As a result, practice for the search subject should include recalling to a whistle, turning on voice or hand signals, etc. Search training without game is acceptable if there are no options but to encourage great search scores, game should be available either planted or naturally present. The more the dog finds game, the better its search becomes.

Pointing (§§ 79-80)

To get the highest score in Pointing, a dog must be "staunch". This means steady and still as the handler approaches in a calm manner and could have shot the game without haste. Of course, dogs that avoid game ("blinkers") will fail and be removed from the test. Blinkers almost invariably come from too much e-collar stimulation encouraging compliance to the Whoa command. Use of the e-collar around game requires extreme caution. At this level, we are looking for finished pointing dogs. They must also be steady to both wing and shot although this is actually scored under the Obedience subject and will be addressed in a few pages.

The old saw among dog trainers is that they can teach any dog to point and that is probably true. In my experience, the vast majority of DD's will eventually just start pointing as they are exposed to more and more game and that is my basic training regime: put them in a lot of birds and let them learn that pointing is the game. But, most of us want to encourage pointing in a more structured format.

It is a long-standing tradition among bird dog trainers to instill the Whoa command as dogs begin to point. Typically, this command is taught in the yard after a young dog has been in lots of birds and is bird crazy but is actually pointing. This was covered in Chapter 5 in detail. If you stop and think about it, all a dog has to do to enable you to kill birds with it is to "stop on scent". Sure, we want a stylish intense point but you can have a lot of success if the dog just stops when it smells birds. So, our goal is to teach the dog to, in fact, stop and stand still even after the flush and shot.

You can determine that you've taught the Whoa command when you can stand twenty feet from the dog, give the command Whoa and toss a dummy which he will not break for. To prove this, stand about twenty feet away and toss the dummy so that the dog must run by you to get it. Then, if the dog breaks, grab it as it runs by and replace it with emphasis on the original spot. Steadiness to wing, shot, and fall is merely an extension of the Whoa/Halt command and, if practiced many, many times while hunting or training be become instilled without a voice or whistle command.

Manners Behind Game and Relocating

For a good score in this subject, the dog must be able to handle moving game, i.e. birds without flushing them. While there may be some secret tool that will teach a dog this trait, it really just comes down to exposure to lots and lots of birds. The versatile breeds are intelligent animals. If they have been on enough birds, they will learn to elegantly move and eventually pin the birds. The only way to get a dog to this level is lots of hunting. Care should be used in "nicking" dogs with the e-collar if they begin to crowd the moving birds during training. This can lead to blinking which can destroy a good bird dog. A sharp verbal "Ahhnt" might work better in this scenario if they have learned that corrective command.

Searching and Retrieving Shot Game Birds (§82-84)

The German system of dog evaluation puts more emphasis on "after the shot" than before the shot. As a result, retrieving of shot birds is a crucial part of the a versatile dog's training and performance appraisal at a test.

There are four methods the judges can use for determining a dog's ability in this subject but only two will be used at an individual test. First, the judges can attempt to "wing" a bird or ask the handler to shoot at a bird and, if winged, send the dog for tracking it and retrieval. Due to the difficulty in accomplishing this test set-up, it is rarely used in North America. Instead, the vast majority of tests will provide a "drag" of a dead feathered game bird, typically a duck or pheasant. The task is designed to mimic a situation whereby a hunter shot a game bird and the game ran off on the ground after being wounded. A judge will take the bird which you provide and drag it at least 200 meters across a field where he will drop the duck and hide himself in some nearby cover. The scent line will have two obtuse angles in it. While this task is listed under Field Work (and will occur in a field), it is a similar format to the furred drags employed in the Forest and the same format for training are appropriate.

In addition to the Feathered Drag, VGP dogs are required to find a freshly shot bird that the dog did not see fall **(§81-b)**. The judges can either use a freshly shot game bird; usually shot by another handler, to test the dog's ability to search freely, find and retrieve a freshly shot bird much like occurs in nearly every hunting outing. Or, they can merely place a shot, dead bird in some cover and ask the handler to send his dog on an independent search for the bird. In the vast majority of tests, this latter approach will be used. Handlers tend to miss birds if the first format is used and time can become an issue if this goes on and on. So, most of the time, one can anticipate the Free Search and Retrieving of a Placed Bird as the task at hand. The judges will place a dead bird, usually a duck or pheasant, in some fairly dense cover so that the dog can only find it via its nose as opposed to seeing it. The Rule Book states that this cover must be at least 80 meters wide. The judge who places the bird will do so with the wind at his or her back and leave via the same path to avoid the dog simply tracking him to the bird. Of course, the dog will be out of sight as this preparation is done.

Once the bird is in place and the judges have gathered, the handler will be shown the approximate location of the bird from about 50 meters away. He will send his dog on an independent search and the dog must find the bird and must retrieve it to hand. The handler can walk along behind the dog and assist him lightly with encouragement. The dog is expected to hunt closely and show that he is, in fact, using his nose to find the bird. Technically, the Rule Book states that the judges "can end the work of the dog if they think that the dog does satisfy the demands of the task". Does that mean if the dog searches diligently and uses his nose but fails to find the duck, it can score well? Probably not as the Rule Book clearly states in two places in bold print that the dog must find and retrieve the game in this task. Realistically, most dogs perform this task without issue. But, like all the subjects, it should be practiced multiple times before the test.

Manner of Retrieve

Like all retrieves, the dog should approach the handler with the game correctly gripped, sit without a harsh command (again, a gentle, quiet "Sit" or hand signal is acceptable) and freely give the game up to the handler. Some judges consider a hand signal and a quiet "Sit" as one command while others count it as two. It's best to just use one. Despite the straight-forward format, many dogs receive low scores in their Manner. It doesn't matter if the dog comes straight to you and sits or goes around you in the classic retriever style to deliver at your side. The straight-to-the-front method requires a few less steps and a somewhat lower chance of the dog dropping the animal, so that is preferable. Some dogs, even ones that have been trained well, get possessive of an animal, especially a duck they have chased for twenty minutes. They want to parade around with it and show it off. Who could blame them! But, for a finished hunting dog, that is not allowed. Work hard on this Manner business because, even though it is averaged with all your Manner of Retrieves, and only is a multiplier of "1", those points add up and can lead to a Prize I.

To receive a Prize I, a dog must have a "Good" predicate in Nose and Pointing, and at least a "Sufficient" in the other four Field subjects for a total Field Score of 85 points. Prize II is awarded if the dog has at least 70 points in the Field and a Prize III dog will have 55 points in this subject.

Obedience

There are EIGHT subjects in the Obedience Subject! As a result, obedience is crucial for the VGP candidate and, really, there is no excuse for not preparing a dog in this subject. Regardless of weather or time availability, there is always time for obedience training. In fact, the Rule Book states (**§87**) that "obedience during the test therefore has the highest priority among all performances expected". While the judges will be focused on your dog during its actual evaluation during a specific subject, they will also occasionally observe the dog while it is <u>not</u> working. For all practical purposes, your dog will be under evaluation from the time it exits your vehicle until the test is completed. Certainly, the ability of the handler to leash their dog after a subject has been completed will be closely evaluated.

Driven Hunt (§ 91) Verhalten auf dem Stand

During this subject, all the dogs in the test will be lined up, normally on a forest road, while a number of hunters, i.e. the gallery and a judge, will walk through the nearby cover making noise, shooting guns, and generally trying to "drive" game from the cover. In addition, 2 shots will be fired from behind the dog either by the handler or often by one of the judges. For the highest score, the dog must remain totally silent and calm. No whining, barking, pulling on the leash will be allowed and no command may be given by the handler (after the "drive" begins). You have two options: place the dog unleashed and down or on a leash. If you elect to keep the dog leashed, your highest score will be "Good" i.e. a "3".

This is a stressful test for most dogs so it needs to be practiced many times prior to the test. Say, there are four dogs in your group. Each handler will shoot two times plus the judge doing the "driving" will shoot at least once. That's 12 shotgun blasts that your dog must ignore for all practical purposes. No whining, no barking, and certainly no bolting. You can keep the leash on the dog for an automatic "3" or just put the dog down and hope for a "4". That's what I recommend. The problem is that you often don't have a group of people to practice with so take every opportunity when training with a group to apply the requirements for this test. The electronic collar is an excellent tool during this pre-test observation as well as a sharp verbal correction. The dog must be solid on this task for the highest score so drill it regularly.

Heeling on Leash (§92) Leinführigkeit

During this subject the judges will instruct you to walk with your dog on leash through some wooded area, typically winding around trees for 3-5 minutes.   The dog will be required to avoid tangling the leash in the saplings and, if that happens, your score can decrease. Keep in mind, the judges will be casually observing your dog all during the two-day test for problems with leash heeling. There is no reason to get less than a "4" in this subject. There is always time to practice this simple heeling exercise. No commands should be given to the dog during this subject except maybe one soft "Heel" as you begin. The leash should be slack and your hands off the leash. This is why a true Jaeger-type leash is important. For the best score, keep your hands in your pockets and your mouth quiet and practice, practice, practice.

Heeling Off Leash(§93) Folgen frei bei Fuss

Typically, the judges will ask you to heel your dog off leash down a forest road. The Rule Book says no "loud" commands which implies one could give a soft command or two. Regardless, if you think you need to remind your dog of the "Heel" command, be very subtle with it. This subject is designed to mimic a hunting situation whereby you are sneaking up on game. As a result, loud commands would be undesirable. The required distance is 50 meters, so practice heeling off leash at least that far in preparation. You will doubtlessly be asked to jog, then stop suddenly, begin again at a varying pace so be sure your dog understands the requirements. Regular practice is the key with quick correction for lax performance.

The Down Stay (§94) Ablegen

This is an interesting and somewhat challenging subject. The handler walks with his dog (the Rule Book says off leash) to a spot designated by the judges. Typically, this Subject follows the Heeling Off Leash. It will be an isolated spot away from the gallery and awaiting dogs. The handler gives the command to "Down" (in a quiet manner) and walks off as if stalking some big game animal. When the handler has gone at least 30 meters, where a judge will normally be waiting and the dog cannot see either the handler or the judge, two shotgun shots are fired at least 10 seconds apart. The dog must not leave his or her position and you cannot give another command! Nor can he whine or bark.

Now, you can leave something with the dog, e.g. a knapsack or a hunting vest. There is no penalty for this but if you leave a leash on the dog (not tied to the tree!), you can only get a "Good" i.e. a "3" out of the subject.

Ideally, the dog will lie completely down during the entire subject but if he sits up, normally, there is no lowering of the score. The dog can pass this subject as long as he does not move over 5 meters from the original place but his score will probably drop a predicate or two. Keep in mind; the judges are looking for a calm dog in a hunting mode during this subject.

In my experience, the best way to train for this is with an assistant holding an electronic collar transmitter. The assistant hides away from the dog but where the dog can be totally viewed. As the handler walks off after giving the Sit or Halt/Down command, the assistant will correct the dog if it performs poorly. Remember, the dog must remain stationary until the handler returns to the dog so practice the total package, i.e. the dog remains still until you return all the way to it, during training.

Steadiness to Wing (§ 95) Benehmen vor eräugtem Federwild

A dog that remains still as birds flush and a shot is fired and the game falls, is a truly finished bird dog. True, many serious bird hunters do not consider this a major issue rationalizing that if a dog "breaks" as the birds get up, they are quicker to the downed game making retrieving easier and quicker. It is really a moot point for VGP handlers because the dog is required to be "steady" at this test for the initial flush, on the shot and, lately, as the bird drops too. Sponsoring organizations vary around this bird shooting deal. Some never shoot the bird so the Steady to Fall is not required while some will actually shoot the bird.

To make it more interesting, the dog should remain stationary without a command from the handler! Since the dog is also required to be steady to shot **(§98)**, one might as well train for all three simultaneously. The Rule Book also calls for Steadiness to Fur **(§96-97)** but there is an out if there is no "fur" available. To complete the VGP test, a dog must be steady on either birds or fur but not both. Regardless, a complete hunting dog must be controllable to the extent that if it chases fur, e.g. a deer, off it must stoppable. In fact, if the dog fails to come back promptly or cannot be stopped on command, it can fail the test. So, even if there is no test for fur steadiness per se, you should be able to stop your dog from running deer with a whistle blast or loud verbal command. Judicious use of the electronic collar is key here.

Now, about this steadiness business: Steadiness on shot, flush and fall is just an extension of the Whoa command. When solidified over the two or three hunting seasons, it should be dependable at the VGP test. In my experience, dogs can be made steady fairly easily but tend to forget this training unless it is re-enforced each season. Typically, hunters become lax after passing the VGP and let the dog get away with movement after the flush or shot. In fact, many hunters prefer their dog not be so steady. But, for the VGP, strict adherence to the Whoa command prior to the test (you can't give the command at the test) will insure a good score in this subject.

Since the final training for the VGP occurs in the summer, often classic game birds, e.g. quail, are unavailable. Pigeons are a nice tool but you can go through a lot of pigeons if you shoot them to solidify the steadiness to fall bit. I use a Dokken duck to get this going in the right direction. Sit the dog at your side, toss (or have someone else toss) the fake duck high in the air, shoot the gun (not at the duck!) and let it fall. Then, send for the retrieve. If the dog breaks, correct it with the training collar. While this mimics a waterfowl blind situation, the format transitions well to upland hunting too. The dog learns that it cannot move until released. After several weeks of practice, the command becomes solid.

Additionally, the pallet with a stake driven at one corner is a nice tool. A ten foot chain or rope is firmly attached and a JASA collar added. Toss a bird out in front of the dog and as it bolts for it, just as it reaches the end of its rope, so to speak, nick it with the collar and say Whoa.

Hopefully, one can get into the upland field for a few hunts before the VGP and reinforce the command on actual flushing and falling birds. At many VGP tests, dogs that are totally steady to wing, shot, and fall are unusual. In many instances, if the handler can just stop the dog with a verbal or whistle command, the dog will pass albeit with a lower score. One tactic that can be used and is fairly easy to accomplish is just train the dog to Halt on a gun shot. As the birds get up, a quick shot will stop the dog if it has been trained to do so. Over several weeks, the dog will learn that it cannot move unless released even as a bird falls. The shot is the command. This is fine but one must advise the judges during the Gun Sensitivity portion of the test about this training tactic. Otherwise, they might think the dog is gun sensitive if it lies down on a shot during the search or Gun Sensitivity evaluation. In my experience, heavy training around steadiness and/or Halt can deteriorate a dog's search substantially. Be careful with dog's that do not have a great search to begin with. Dogs with a lot of drive and great searchers do better with this training strategy.

You have probably said Whoa a hundred times over the summer and it is very easy for the command to slip out at the test. Stay focused and just don't say it.

For a Prize I, the dog must get at least a "sufficient" in the Drive Hunt, Heeling on Leash and Heeling Off Leash and Down Stay and a total of 43 points

For a Prize II, the dog must be at least "sufficient" on the Drive Hunt and Heeling on Leash and 40 points.

For a Prize III, the dog must again be at least "sufficient" on the Drive Hunt and Heeling on Leash but only needs 38 points in this category

Some Final Tips

1. Dress the part. Sure, you want to be dressed for the weather but traditionally, loden shades are the standard. In the U.S., hunter orange is common and a splash of orange is fine but be subtle. Some handlers wear a white shirt like the retriever folks do to help their dog find them after a drag which is OK. Wear the same clothes that you train in. Your dog picks up on that.
2. Have a jaeger lead. This shows preparation and really it is handy for all the Subjects in the VGP.
3. Wear your whistle. While you don't need to tweet the thing continually, it is nice to have available. Please don't show up at a test without a whistle and yell "Here" to your dog. These are not a pack of hounds you are hunting.
4. Be organized. Especially around game management before and during the test. Have your paperwork in order. Fill out the Formblat 1 (the entry form) correctly and put a note in the envelope with your email address on it so the Test Director can communicate with you easily.
5. Relax as much as possible. Dogs pick up on the nervousness of their owner/handler. Use the term "Good Boy" or "Good Girl" regularly in training and the day of the test, this phrase can be a calming tool. Bond with your dog daily. Lots of petting and praise. The dog needs to like you; not fear you. On test day, just before a Subject, give that petting and "Good Boy/Girl" to assure the dog that everything is OK.
6. Let the dog mouth and hold drag game the day before the test and rub your hands all over the game to allow the dog to recognize its personal duck or rabbit or fox or raccoon.
7. If you don't have handy water duck searches on land are good too. I don't do real duck searches the two weeks before the test but might turn a live flightless duck loose in a field or even a large lawn; let it wander off so you can send the dog on a tracking/searching exercise. They will find the duck and bring it back to you with lots of enthusiasm. It's fun to do and helps some too.
8. If there are hazards in the Search Water (sticks, stumps, and hidden objects) you might consider removing the collar from the dog prior to this Subject. But, if you are going to do this, please practice releasing the dog without its collar. To try and do this on test day breaks the dog's concentration and the daily training routine is lost.
9. Between Subjects, relax and talk to your dog continually bonding and encouraging.

Test Day

Day Before: Recheck your Check List around gear. Decide about your game, especially your foxes/raccoons/rabbits. When should you start to thaw them? Ducks are less of an issue. Are you going to be able to get everything in one cooler? Heck, do you even have a cooler? Plan all this days ahead of the test.

Arrive at the testing area the afternoon before the test. Get your dog out and let it adjust to the fields and water. No real training needs to be done at this point. Just let them get used to the environment.

Feed the dog as early as possible, say 3-4 PM, provide plenty of water. If you think your dog needs extra energy, provide a top dressing of a product like K9 Restart (www.tech-mix.com) on the food. Both of you go to bed early.

Be at the test site at the appointed time but with enough interval to allow light "airing out". Dress appropriately of course around the weather but have rain gear, extra boots, etc. in your truck. Over a two-day test, anything can happen.

Present the dog's paperwork to the Test Director and stand back. By mid-morning, give your dog a "boost" using one of the products made for this or, better, a handful of dog food in a pan. This is often the best supplement available. Don't overdo it….just a cup. You don't want to weight the dog down with a big meal. Skipping ahead, feed the dog the first afternoon as soon as possible after the testing has concluded.

Remain calm and pace yourself mentally all day long. Act like it is something you've done before even if you are nervous.

The VGP scoring system is based on a 4 point maximum so for the judges to ding you to a lower predicate, they have to decrease their evaluation by 25%…that's a lot. Unless there's a glaring issue and if your dog is well-prepared, you will get plenty of "4's". Many judges will be watching your dog from the time the test starts until the end even if you and your dog are not the dog testing in the Subject. Obedience will be monitored all day long.

If you Fail, don't worry. The dog is doubtlessly a fine hunting dog and better than the vast majority of sporting dogs. If you Pass, accept the accomplishment gracefully and then celebrate with the other Utility Dog owners.

Chapter Eleven: Getting Someone Else To Do It

I have tried it both ways: training my dog myself and paying someone to do it. Both have worked. But, there are very few trainers in North America that are truly "versatile" trainers. The bird dog guy won't fool with retrieving and certainly not rabbits. The retriever trainer won't do the pointing. And, all the obedience stuff is just too much for the average, down-the-street dog trainer. After going through several dogs, I guess my position is I'd rather have a mediocre dog I trained myself than a great dog someone else trained. But, if you are really short on spare time and can afford it, finding one of the rare versatile trainers is an option.

I think is OK is to pay someone to FF the dog. Now, optimally, you do it yourself because this regime builds a relationship with the dog that only you will have and this is a wonderful benefit. I admit I have had decent luck letting someone else FF my dog. But, I have also been disappointed. See, the pure retriever trainer is looking for a somewhat different dog than we are as versatile dog owners. And, they are in the business of getting them done and through as quickly as possible. There's a tendency to rush the project. Plus, if this is their first versatile, they may have preconceived notions about the breed which may be negative resulting in them being too ardent in their approach. Regardless, if the trainer will listen to you about what you want and the dog needs, it can work.

If another person trains your dog for the JGHV tests, you might consider paying this person to handle the dog in the tests. It is challenging for a dog to switch trainers a few weeks before a test but I have done it and it worked out fine. But, I've been there and done it before. This is just something you need to consider. Overall, I recommend you train your own dog. Give the dog two years of training and it will give you ten years of hunting and companionship.

Chapter Twelve: Conditioning

All the JGHV tests require that a dog be "in shape" but the VGP is especially demanding due to the two-day duration. Conditioning a dog breaks into two components: physical and mental.

There are many ways to physically condition a dog but the underpinning is aerobic exercise, i.e. running. Dogs burn calories much more efficiently than humans. Sled dogs reportedly burn up to 15,000 calories per day during competition. You cannot jog with the dog enough to truly condition it aerobically. A vehicle of some type is required. Professional bird dog trainers use an ATV with a wide bar attached and short leashes for the dog as they drive around conditioning 4-6 dogs at a time. This is optimal because it not only builds aerobic endurance but also forces the dog to pull against the ATV's resistance building muscle mass in the important back and leg muscles. But, for the one dog versatile trainer, this device is probably too much sugar for a dime as they say. Rather, just running alongside your ATV or hunting cart is fine. Starting slow, 3-4 miles per hour and for just a mile or so, gradually build the dog's stamina to a 3 miles level at about 6-7 miles per hour. Create a course in your training area and gradually build up to 3 times per week before the test or the beginning of hunting season.

Nutrition is an important component of physical conditioning of the athletic dog. If the dog has been on the "easy list" all summer (no training or hunting) and you've been feeding a maintenance food, switch to a "performance" food about eight weeks before beginning training or hunting season. This means a "30/20" matrix; 30% protein and 20% fat. There are several brands of food that offer this type product. It takes about 8 weeks for the little fuel burning part of the muscle cell, call the mitochondria, to adjust and utilize the newer food. For performance, fat is the key ingredient because fat has 9 times the calories than protein or carbohydrates (grain). So, a dog gets a lot more energy from a bite of high-fat food allowing you to feed the normal *amount* of food while supplying optimal energy for the dog. How much to feed? That depends on the dog. Read your dog not the dog food bag label which provides mere guidelines. I want to feel the ribs but not see them and I want a true waist on the dog just in front of those rear legs.

Protein levels are important too. Research studies have documented that dogs on higher protein levels in their food have less soft-tissue injuries even on foods with 18% protein amounts. Thus, the 30% protein level is recommended.

Feeding times are important too. My Dad routinely kept our dogs on an empty stomach the night before a big hunt. I thought this was crazy but it turns out that dogs hunted on an empty stomach actually increases stamina the next day up to 100%; totally opposite of our intuition. Certainly, feeding the dog an hour or so before the test is a bad idea. Ideally, dogs are fed as soon as possible after hunting, training or testing. This means right after you get back to your camp, home or motel and before you fix a cocktail or take a shower. The reason is two-fold. First, the sooner the dog is fed, the sooner the ingesta/poop can move through the GI tract. We don't want to hunt a dog that has a full gut which causes some biomechanical sloshing around which slows the dog. Plus, the colon can get irritated with a lot of food in it while hunting leading the common diarrhea seen with high energy hunting dogs. Secondly, this early feeding allows the dog to assimilate the nutrition especially the energy source, get the insulin spike that results out of the way and let it return to normal prior to activity. If a dog is fed late at night or first thing in the morning, this increase in insulin can block the surge of energy needed for the test or a hard hunt.

What about these magic supplements that are available for hard hunting dogs? Generally, they are not needed. Sure, you can give a high-fat snack like a piece of wiener or sausage mid-morning (the insulin spike won't have time to interfere that quickly). It is true that after a hard morning in the field, the dog's energy levels can be depleted so some products called "glucose polymers" can give a quick post-exercise boost. The best known one is maltodextrin. There are a number of products available for dogs that contain maltodextrin. Just do an Internet search for "maltodextrin for dogs" to see what's out there.

Of course, keeping the dog hydrated is crucial. There are some special methods for increasing hydration using a product called glycerol but it is complicated and has some downsides. Consult with your local veterinarian about its use but, for the vast majority of versatile hunters, just providing plenty of fresh, clean water is adequate. A water bottle carried in your vest in the field is almost a no-brainer and should be along on every training, testing or hunting venture.

Mental conditioning is almost as important as physical exercise. Traveling long distances to a test or a hunt with the dog cooped in a dog trailer or kennel is stressful and some dogs will shut down over a period of days. I recommend taking the dog on a non-hunting walk in a relaxed manner, letting the dog ride up front with you for a few hours, or even just a day's rest to allow it to recuperate mentally. At a test, like the VGP, quiet time between subjects, lots of petting and praise, and a treat all along can keep the dog focused.

Chapter Thirteen: So, You Want to Be a Breeder?

Developing a breeding program is a labor of love. The project requires hours of planning, preparation, and diligence. This is not the same as "raising a litter". The scenario is common: a person buys their first versatile dog; it's a female, and she does well in the JGHV tests. And, she makes a good hunting dog. The owner, in love with the dog and thinking about all the expense they incurred during the testing process, decides "Hey, I can sell some puppies!" Alas, while the dog is a fine dog, in the big scheme of the breed, she is just average. See, almost all the dogs in the versatile breeds will make excellent hunting dogs if exposed to training and game. But, there are few truly outstanding dogs. These are the ones that deserve breeding if we are going to have true breed improvement over decades. Just because a dog is "Certified for Breeding" by their breed organization it doesn't mean that they should be bred.

If you stop and think about it, very few hunters actually <u>need</u> a versatile hunting dog. According to the U. S. Fish and Wildlife Service, about 6% of the American public hunts. Of those, most are big game hunters i.e. whitetail deer. Then, you have to pure waterfowlers and the rather scarce pure upland hunter. The group that hunts waterfowl one day, upland birds the next, and tracks wounded deer on the weekend, is tiny. The bottom line is that the market for versatile hunting dogs is miniscule. If every person who owns a versatile hunting dog came to a big meeting; every breed represented, and we all gathered at a major college football stadium......we wouldn't fill up half the seats. Realistically, it is easy to flood the market with our puppies which eventually results in the youngsters going to marginal homes, non-hunters, etc. See, what happens is a litter of say, eight puppies is born. Three of them are sold to versatile hunters and the breeder keeps one. So, four need homes resulting in the breeder being less than selective placing those extra ones. They often end in less than optimal homes. I know of dozens of examples of this scenario. While I don't want to discourage new breeders, I do want to stress the hassle factor and the responsibility incurred with breeding these unique dog breeds. It should not be taken lightly.

Starting a Breeding Program

The first requirement for any attempt at breeding dogs is the selection process. This is a crucial element and can only occur if one actually uses the dogs being considered for a mating as hunters. There are subtle differences in dogs that only the owner will note over months in the field and duck blind. And, kennel blindness is a disease we all have to a degree. To be successful, all breeders must cull ruthlessly even if it means your favorite dog and hunting companion. I don't mean actually getting rid of the dog but just an honest appraisal of its breeding worthiness. It can be challenging.

Selection, per se, requires either actually hunting with stud dogs or, at the least, lots of phone calls to people who have hunted with the dog. Convenience, distance, costs, etc. just have to be secondary parameters. It can get complicated.

Selection, especially around the male, goes much deeper than the dog's individual performance and test scores. The acid test is what his *puppies* have done. Animal breeding is replete with examples of great performers who never sired a decent progeny. Here's a good story to remember....

Dust Commander was the 1970 Kentucky Derby winner. He was bought as a yearling in Kentucky in 1968 for $6,500. He was sired by Bold Commander who in turn was sired by a son of the great Bold Ruler going back to the foundation sire, Nearco. Dust Commander won a few minor races as a 2-year old but was never considered a Derby contender. Few believed in him as he came off at Churchill Downs at 15-1 odds. But, he charged to the finish in the stretch to win by a length. After the Derby, he started 19 more races only winning one. He was considered a fluke and overlooked by almost all Thoroughbred breeders.

Ten months after his derby win, he was retired to stud with a paltry fee of just $1,500 per cover. There was little interest and his owners actually bred several non-descript mares for free. Eventually, he was sold for $500,000 to some Japanese horsemen; relegated to Triple A ball.

A few years passed and Dust Commander's foals began to show up at the racetrack. Foaled by those mediocre mares during his three year stay in Kentucky, there was little fanfare. Remarkably, Dust Commander's progeny had 53 winners, seven of them in stakes races out of just 62 total sons and daughters.

Dust Commander was returned to the U. S. for $6.75 million and his new stud fee was $50,000.[6]

What the moral? It's all about the puppies....not the individual male you are selecting. And, it is important to note that Dust Commander, while a mediocre performer, had a deep pedigree. He wasn't a world beater but he had blood behind him. It is fine to roll the dice with a new, unproven male (someone has to and I have) but a shorter route to fame as a breeder is to select the male based on his puppies' reputation plus the dogs behind him on the back of that Ahnentafel. Some people will tell you the over-use of major stud dogs decreases the gene pool. While this could be true, the reality is that smaller gene pools also allow undesirable recessive traits to rise to the top. So, over decades, it really isn't a bad thing.

As one carefully inspects their female, doubtlessly, there will be a trait that is needed. They all need something! Once the lack is determined, one can breed to "excess" to correct the deficiency. Here's another story: Smokey River Blue Sage was a Bluetick coonhound of the 1960's. He was a fanatic tree dog, barking incessantly when treed. Alas, many times he did this with no game up the tree! This "false treeing" was a real nuisance as the hunter would walk all the way to Sage only to find nothing up the tree. But, Sage came around when hard treeing dogs were scarce in the Bluetick breed so folks bred females to him to get this trait ingrained. The females were not liars but needed more ardent treeing. Sure enough, Sage's progeny became some of the best Blueticks in the breed. This is called "breeding to excess" and can be used to correct needed qualities. [7] But, you have to be able to determine those "needed qualities".

Before one considers developing a breeding program around versatile hunting dogs, months of introspection needs to occur. Do you have the time to study pedigrees, talk to other breeders, go to tests to see puppies perform, and do you have the time to actually attend the whelping and puppy care thereafter? All these questions need to be answered in an honest manner.

To gain recognition as a breeder and to move your breed forward, money has to be a secondary consideration. This means placing puppies in the hands of proven owners, often for free. Established owners, who will train and test the dog and hunt it hard for a few years to determine its innate traits are hard to find. Often, they are involved in their own breeding package. To develop a true strain of hunting dogs using new, inexperienced owners is a spot-on gamble.

As dog breeding goes, breeding versatile hunting dogs that are tested in the JGHV system is a real hassle. In many other breeds and registries, little oversight is required and breeders can breed Ol' Sue to Ol' Joe without concern because if the results are a flub, well, no one notices. In our breeds, lots of paperwork, testing, and certification is required along with peer review by judges to determine the quality of the produced puppies. It is not an easy road; a task not to be taken lightly.

As stated above, the key to success in a canine breeding program is the initial selection process. As Mr. Ormiston says in his book "Life is too short to drink cheap wine." [7]. The good news is that breeders don't have to start from scratch. They can begin with high quality males and females from the beginning. Alas, that high quality individual may or may not be the dog that you currently own. To gain fame, you must breed dogs that, essentially, train themselves because most of your puppy buyers will be newbies without a clue around preparing for JGHV testing. In my experience, about 20% of the puppy buyers actually follow through with breeder recommendations and give your puppy a fair chance so your odds of making a name for yourself are not in your favor. And, along this line, you need to be able to actually provide the correct advice to the new owner. This is hard to do if you have only trained one or two dogs for the required tests.

One could overcome this by producing a large number of puppies annually but current breeding restrictions (a good thing) preclude this method. Or, you could keep all the puppies yourself and select only the very best prospects for actual testing but who is crazy enough to try that?

Most people start their career in versatile dogs with a puppy. Who doesn't like a puppy? Alas, this is the most tortuous route to fame as a breeder. An experienced breeder of versatile dogs told me that he went through eleven puppies before he found one he could hang his hat on. Oh, the puppies were all decent hunting dogs and scored well in the tests. But, finding that special dog that offers a foundation for a breeding program is scarce. A better way would be to purchase a proven adult female that has produced above average puppies. Alas, those kind of females are rarely for sale and if they are, they can get pricey. Regardless, if you put the pencil to it, this is the most economical and sure way to begin.

Successful breeders have a plan. They have a picture of where they want to be ten or even twenty years down the road. Ideally, this is a written plan. Weeks or months are spent developing the plan and the standards for selection. For example, minimal scores in JGHV tests? If she scores 159 at an HZP, will she be included in the breeding program? Passing the VGP? Minimal scores for Coat and Conformation? Overall skill as a hunting dog? Over how many seasons? You get the idea but these criteria need to be set early in the breeding program and, with rare exceptions, held over your lifetime. This is the art of dog breeding. Think "careful breeding". Obviously, the more stringent these standards are, the harder it will be to find a breedable dog. But, over time, a high bar is the only real way to move the Bell Curve to the right. Helter-skelter breeding will result in more failures than successes. You have to have a plan with high standards.

6. Mclin J; Breeding Good Hounds; American Beagler, August 2002
7. Ormiston G; New Guide to Breeding Old Fashioned Working Dogs, 1989

Appendix

Check List for VGP

Your dog	Breech Opening Shotgun
Ahnentafel	Rain Gear
Rabies Certificate	Clothing
Hunting License	Snacks and Beverages
Food and Water for 3 days (for Dog)	Dead Duck(s)
Food and Water Pans	Dead Rabbit(s)
Dead Fox(es) or Raccoon(s)	Drag String
Blood Tracking Collar and Lead	2 Golf Balls
Jager Lead	Cash
Cooler for game	Water bottle for dog
VGPO Rule Book	Folding Chair
Whistle	Cotton balls for marking blood
Kennel for dog	

Dr. Coffman is a graduate, licensed veterinarian in private practice. He has been a Drahthaar owner since 2000; is a Performance Judge, a former Breed Warden for the southeastern United States and owns vom Briermeister Drahthaar kennels.

He has taken three dogs through the VGP.

Made in the USA
Columbia, SC
27 April 2019